WOUNDED

WOUNDED

STEVEN TROY HANSERD

XULON PRESS

Xulon Press
2301 Lucien Way #415
Maitland, FL 32751
407.339.4217
www.xulonpress.com

Paperback ISBN-13: 978-1-66284-133-0
Hard Cover ISBN-13: 978-1-66284-134-7
Ebook ISBN-13: 978-1-66284-135-4

Acknowledgments

I would like to dedicate this book to the three most

important women in my life:

Betty, Palestine and Mary.

You make this world a better place!

I told the Lord "I saw you work in others and I want you

to work in me."

Table of Contents

Introduction

The gift of God so freely fell upon me this morning and the mysteries and puzzles were unlocked for me with one touch from God's hand, things that have perplexed, plagued, as well as, intrigued me all my life.

When Jesus sings, he breathes life into men. I awoke this morning from a dream and the Spirit of God gave me an epiphany, the answer to all my problems: His Holy Word.

If I had known better, I would have been obedient to the Holy Spirit and finished this project long ago. Everything in its own time and season, with patience and perseverance. "We are more than conquerors."

Howbeit, so many reasons for so many setbacks and failures, and the key to unlock the door be right in front of you. Blinded by the light, snow-blind and all kinds of blind. Multiple ways to be blinded, never at the same time or in the same way.

Only hoping for a vision in all ways. A vision that would guide me through this maze I have been trapped in for most of my life.

If I could turn back the sands of time, I'd probably not do so because of all the fantastic things I have experienced in my life. Unforgettable dream making moments! Along with the people I've met along the way.

I'm talking about characters most like myself, with split personalities. Traits adopted and obtained to survive this cold-blooded game. Gifts and dreadful curses used to make it in the trenches of some of the most cutthroat gang and game oriented individuals ever placed on this earth.

A journey surrounded by many, but perpetually isolated on a desolate island. Spinning endlessly in a cycle that horrifyingly has not an end to it.

A painful lesson in life that is on repeat, song after song, chapter after chapter until there is an expelled breath of surrender, realizing that you are only human in a supernatural war. A war that cannot and will not be won in your own strength or on your own.

Millions didn't make it, but I was one of the ones who did. Why? Only by His Grace and calling purposed on my life from the origin of my being. Why? Only because of the many who continue to, even now, be trapped, held hostage and wounded.

In need of the same thing I was afforded time after time; forgiveness and another chance.

I once asked my mother, "How many times was I going to have to keep starting over and trying again? She exclaimed, "You keep trying until you get it right."

In any battle, struggle or addiction you are facing, never give up on yourself. If you lie down, get knocked down, slip and fall and just lay there, the world will roll right over you. If you don't learn to keep fighting, pressing own and believing, no one else will do it for you.

I press onward toward the mark, forgetting those things which are in the past, not driving in the rear view mirror, but one day at a time. Slowly, one step at a time, replacing hopelessness with a brighter future, caring enough about my own life to want to live again, have and enjoy.

I will hold your hand and take you through this story. If it had not been for all the things I went through, I would not be half of the man I am today.

To all those mentioned and not mentioned, you know who you are. Be blessed for your prayers, encouragement and Christian service, dedicated to holding me up when I could not hold myself.

My promise to you is that I am forever indebted to you and promise to always pay it forward, for I will never be able to repay you for all you have done for me.

"We give ourselves to your cause, dedicating our lives to reach the lost. For we may never know all whose lives we've touched with LOVE."

Foreword

by

Joan Adrienne Sturgis

Editor

For African Americans and other people of color who have been incarcerated in the United States, the road to reacclimate back into society can be a long and arduous journey. With time served and the optimism of starting life anew, inmates leaving prison with acquired education and certified training skills, are often met with hostility and resentment from an unforgiving society that strongly believes, former inmates aren't deserving of "any" equal rights.

Having spent four years teaching at the California Institution for Men at Chino, I understand why the potential to reoffend and be re-incarcerated can occur, time and time again. Our government has failed minority communities miserably in resolving important and valid discriminatory issues such as their rights for quality education, decent paying jobs, and affordable and less sub-standard housing, and the availability of mental health programs.

Yet, in the case of author, Steven Troy Hanserd who, by his own admission, never knew poverty, having grown up in a loving, thriving, and successful family environment, one might wonder how he could have ended up on a cycle of recidivism. And, while Steven's crimes cannot be condoned nor swept under the rug, there is plenty of accountability that must also be laid at the doorstep of the extremely flawed United States Justice System.

The government's obsession with systemic racism and allowing a proliferation of drugs and guns to be saturated throughout communities of color, exacerbate an already existence of hopelessness. Our senses and mental health have become so numbed that we see "people who look like us" as the enemy, and we further devastate and kill one another through the sale of deadly "drugs for profit" and use of guns as the government loses no sleep over our losses.

Because our government has also allowed its prison system to reap excessive financial gain through privatization, when you consider the average "up-keep cost" per inmate is $31,286 per year, it doesn't take a "rocket scientist" to figure out why our prisons have become over-populated, warehousing facilities of humanity.

Every year, the United States releases over seven million people from jails and more than 600,000 from prisons. Within three years of their release, two out of three are re-arrested, and more than 44% are reincarcerated within one year of being released. And sadly enough, if children have been left behind, they are the ones who bear the biggest burden; they become "at-risk" to repeating a cycle of incarceration and recidivism that shows no signs of ever ending.

Chapter 1

In The Beginning

I was born Steven Troy Williams, to William Shelby and Betty R. Williams on June 8, 1970, at Rockford Memorial Hospital in Rockford, Illinois.

While I know very little about what happened to William, following my birth, when I became old enough to understand, I was told that he had a drug problem that negatively impacted our father/son relationship that never had a chance to grow from the start. But, as fate would have it, when my mother met and eventually married Carl L. Hanserd, who adopted me as his son, Carl became the only father I had ever truly known.

Of Carl and Betty's three sons, I am the eldest, followed by my two younger brothers, Dion, and Nicholas. I also have an older brother, Michael, and a sister, Treece, who happens to be my same age), by way of William Shelby.

Early, in my life, I was blessed to have a godfamily who were very influential in my upbringing. My godfamily consists of my godparents, George, and Minnie Lomax, my two godbrothers, George, Jr., and James, and my four godsisters, Collette, Marilyn, Patricia, and Lisa. As parental surrogates, the Lomax family will forever be an intricate part of my upbringing, just as they continue their support of me today.

While I intend no disrespect to William, simply because his absence in my life is what it is, Carl is who I choose to recognize as "dad" or "my father" throughout my story. Carl was the one who coached me in Little League Basketball and got me involved in Junior Tackle Football and Little League Baseball. Dad's very hands-approach and patience to teach me everything I would come to learn about each sport, sparked a passion in me about athletics that carried over into my adult life.

Although my mom was supportive of my interest in sports, she had a passion of her own.

It was shopping. Whenever I could, I loved to tag along. She would get us up early on a Saturday morning, and we would be gone all day. Joining us on her "shop 'til you drop" excursions would usually be my Aunt Jerri or one of my mom's girlfriends.

Some might say that I was spoiled as I was growing up, because I never wanted for anything, and I was never neglected. For the longest, I enjoyed being the only child but, when Dion and Nick came along, I was so proud to be their big brother.

The home of my grandfather, Arthur Williams (Daddy) and grandmother, Justine Williams (MaDear), who resided on Lincoln Avenue in Rockford, served as the family's headquarters, as well as my home away from home.

I usually spent all my time at my grandparents' home, playing with my younger cousin, Erica. I remember doing chores for my grandmother, which I loved, because she would pay us fifty cents or a dollar for helping her around the house. Then, with money in hand, we would run to the corner store to buy an assortment of penny candy or to The Dariette on Montague and Central Avenue for ice cream on a humid and hot day.

We had a great childhood growing up on Lincoln Avenue. In my mind, the memories of those carefree days will always be my safe place to retreat whenever things become their worst for me.

I often remember spinning around and around on a kitchen stool as I watched MaDear magically create a "soul food" meal that would, somehow, be enough to feed a small army. But it was prohibited for anyone to enter MaDear's home without taking off their hat or washing their hands. MaDear loved watching us make our plates and always encouraged us to help ourselves to an extra-large bounty of God's love.

When it came to MaDear loving her family and people, in general, she loved like no other person I've ever encountered in my life. She didn't care who you were or where you were from, and she cared even less about whatever you had previously done or what your present situation happened to be. She had nothing but the utmost of wisdom and unconditional love for everyone, and it was those qualities that endeared her to everyone.

I remember on those nights when it would be just the two of us in MaDear's bedroom. She would patiently read the Bible to me, so that I could learn the order of books in both the Old and New Testaments, along with their many scriptures. Then, before calling it a night, we would watch the late-night news on WTVO, followed by the Johnny Carson Show. I can honestly say, without a doubt, that MaDear will be the most God-like person that I will have ever encountered during my time on earth.

My grandfather, Arthur, who we affectionately called "Daddy" was a quiet man and an avid fisherman, who liked to drink and take long road trips. And although you would rarely catch him at a church service on Sundays, he never failed in sending his tithes and offerings.

"Daddy" was the unheralded foundation of our family. Everything we had, he worked hard for. It is said that during the forty years he worked on the same job, he never missed a day's work.

Now, my grandparents had dozens of grandchildren, but I liked to believe that I was their favorite grandchild, because I always spent the most time with them when I was younger.

My father's mother, Odessa Hanserd (Granny) and his father, Lewis Hanserd (PawPaw) also lived in Rockford on a big hill on Ogilby Road. Granny was a loving woman, who also filled her home with the love of God, along with love for her entire family.

Now Granny made some of the most incredible pineapple cakes and peach cobblers from scratch, and then she would make batches of homemade ice cream, that often found us fighting and arguing over who would get the last slice or scoop of whatever was left.

PawPaw had a big garden that he planted, yearly, high on a hill in the backyard. When he wasn't tending to his assorted vegetables, he would hold his arms out for us to come sit on his lap. He would then trick us by putting our small hands in his, and he would squeeze our fingers and tickle us until we could barely breathe as we laughed hysterically.

Sadly, there's not much I remember about PawPaw because, when I was quite young, he died from cancer. What I do remember, however, is as our grandfather laid in that casket at the front of the church, just feet from where we sat, my cousin, Duntai, and I cried and cried, because we realized that he would no longer be a part of our lives. Yet, after PawPaw's death, somehow and amazingly, life on Ogilby Road continued as usual.

When PawPaw was still alive, we had the most magical Christmases, at his and Granny's house. Every year, Duntai and I would get the exact same toys, gifts, and clothing, among the literally hundreds of presents wrapped under that big ole silver aluminum tree. There was always something special for everyone but, more importantly, everyone always received exactly what they wanted.

As my brothers and I got older, our parents eventually moved us to a small home at 1836 Loomis Street. Our new neighborhood had a lot of families with kids our age and, 'Levings Lake,' which was within walking distance, served as the center point of attraction, from May to October, for such fun-filled activities as family picnics in any one of three shelters, and fishing from a well-stocked lake filled with bass and catfish.

Mom and Dad started leaving me in charge to watch over my younger brothers and the house during the day, while they both worked full-time. During those days, Dion, Nick, and I never had a dull moment. We were closer than the Three Musketeers, and we stuck together, no matter what! However, by being the oldest and feeling like I was "the boss," I bullied and picked on them, mercilessly, simply for fun. I would even bribe and con them as most big brothers do, yet I loved them more than anything else.

One thing I loved to do was cook breakfast and lunch for Dion and Nick. Mom always made sure there was plenty of food for us, and I would experiment cooking things that, somehow, managed to usually come out just right.

Once our stomachs were full, the three of us would spend the day playing endless hours of baseball, listening to Chicago radio stations on cable, and watching cartoons and music videos. Then, once we were bored with that, we would wrestle, fight, and get into any and everything that we knew we weren't supposed to be doing.

My brothers and I got lost in our own world; safe from life's real issues and not having anything to worry about, at all. And although we were much too young to know it at the time, years later, I came to realize that we were truly blessed beyond measure.

Chapter 2

Early One Sunday Morning

I t was an early Sunday morning, and Mom had cooked our favorite breakfast of grits, sausage, cheese-eggs, and biscuits, along with MaDear's famous pear preserves. A hearty breakfast was routine before preparing to head out to church for Sunday school. In our family, staying at home was not an option. Fortunately, I never considered going to Sunday school as a painful event, because I knew all my friends, cousins, and the girls I liked would be there as well.

My upbringing in a traditional Baptist church gave me what I later found to be an advantageous foundation in building my character, ethics and integrity. I can't deny the fact that, among my peers, I was special with the elders of the church. They fastened their eyes upon my young life and instilled in me every spiritual gift they could offer.

I loved going to church so much that I began singing in the choir, became a junior deacon, and looked forward to reciting holiday speeches that my mom and dad enjoyed hearing.

Once I got to high school, however, like most teenagers, I became rebellious and there was little that anyone could tell me. As time gradually passed, little by little, I shied away from the church.

At school, I met a girl named Stephanie. She and her brother, who was a friend of mine, were in my science class. I had been paying close attention to Stephanie, hoping to hook up with her and, eventually, I asked her brother to introduce me to her.

At the time, I was fourteen and Stephanie was sixteen. We hit it off immediately then, shortly after, we started skipping school a lot just so we could be together. Eventually, when Stephanie ended up getting pregnant, I was so scared to death of how my mom would react that I kept it quiet for as long as I could. Then, nine months later, after turning fifteen, Steph and I became parents of a daughter we named Ceara.

Momma had constantly been telling me to slow down, but her warnings were too late. My desires for sex, alcohol, and marijuana overpowered my good sense and left me consumed with the pursuit of pleasure.

Because I was already athletically inclined, it seemed natural that I should play sports in school. My other extra-curricular activities included playing the saxophone and the clarinet and, for a while, I participated in the Band class. I made every effort to keep my grades up and worked part-time to help support myself and my daughter, who was and has always been my twin and my heart.

So, here I was... a "baby" with a baby, but that didn't mean my mother was about to be any easier on me. She was as strict as ever, if not more. In the middle of the night, I would sneak out of my bedroom window to be with Stephanie. This went on for quite some time until my mother discovered what I was doing and confronted me; putting an end to my nightly escapades.

Stephanie eventually moved into low-income housing, and we continued with our adolescent relationship for another year or so. And, while I loved Steph, the truth is we were both too young to ever stand a real chance at having any kind of productive life together.

Not long after our relationship ended, I started dating a very pretty and intelligent, young girl named Lori, who I met at church. Lori and I began spending a lot of time together and, before we knew it, we had fallen deeply in love. I felt so proud being Lori's boyfriend and cherished spending as much time as I could with her.

Although Lori was very naive when it came to "the streets," I wasn't bothered by that because our relationship was more dimensional. It was very romantic and frequently turned intellectual as she patiently taught me about the use of correct English, vocabulary, grammar, and pop music.

During the time I was growing up, I had three best friends, Duntai, Little Stevie and Reggie. As our bonds grew tighter, we became as close as blood brothers. We did just about everything together and spent every moment away from our homes with one another; rain, snow, sleet, or shine.

Then one day, while we were sitting around, we came up with the idea of forming a gospel group. We called ourselves "Future." By the time my dad finally heard us, we were pretty "doggone" tight. Now, my dad was and still is a seasoned singer, himself, so it was only natural that he would take over the coordination of our vocals. As we perfected our three-part harmony, we could easily hold our own against the best of any other singers out there.

We dreamed of becoming famous and performed at various gospel attractions and concerts throughout the city. At one point, we even hosted our own concert that featured us on the marquee, and we were a huge success.

Since we all were firm believers in God and served Him through song in our collective ministry, I began to lead our group through scripture references and prayer to build a stronger foundation for our spirituality as we served Him through song. Through our faith and persistent drive, "Future" quickly took on the persona of Christian rock stars around town, and we became popular among the youth in our community.

Not to be outdone, however, our girlfriends, Lori, Yolanda and Jamecia, who collectively could "blow the roof off" of the church, formed a group, called "Ladies of Christ."

As you will see in my story as it continues to unfold, the only thing constant in life is change. If everything stayed the same, life would be perfect; but, seasons change, people change, and as the late soulful songwriter Bernard Ighner wrote, 'Everything Must Change; Nothing stays the same.'

Chapter 3

From Boys to Men

After squeaking past high school, I immediately joined the Navy on my eighteenth birthday. I just had to get away from home. Now, don't get me wrong, my parents were great. They didn't drink, smoke or gamble. They both had decent paying, full-time jobs, and they did all they could to give my brothers and I the best chance of being the men they prayed we would grow into being.

Lori and I were an item and she loyally supported, encouraged, and waited for me to finish Boot Camp, so we could resume our life together.

After graduating from Boot Camp, I was sent to a technical training school in Millington, Tennessee, about thirty minutes outside of Memphis, where my Aunt Pat was living. Trained as a Jet Engine Mechanic, I studied very hard and exercised like a fanatic throughout the school weeks. Then, every weekend, I would go to Memphis to stay with Aunt Pat.

Mid-way through my training, I flew Lori down to Memphis to spend the weekend with me. While she was there, I surprised her with a small engagement ring, asked her to marry me, and she said 'yes.' Now that we were happily engaged, there was no end to the dreams that Lori and I shared about finally building a life together.

When I eventually graduated from technical school in the top three of my class, I was ordered to be on a squadron that was assigned to the USS Nimitz nuclear aircraft carrier that was already on a western Pacific tour. Immediately, I had to ship out and meet its 6,012-member crew on the other side of the world.

From Chicago's O'Hare Airport, it took a three-day flight to reach the Indian Ocean, outside of Saudi Arabia. From the moment I boarded the Nimitz, one of the world's largest warships in the world, it became "all work and no play" as I began my seafaring career.

Every evening at sundown, I would walk up to the flight deck, all alone, and watch the most beautiful sunsets I had ever seen. As the sun seemingly dropped over the edge of the earth, I envisioned and prayed for my family and Lori back in the states.

Working on the flight deck of an aircraft carrier was exciting, but also dangerous.   I went through rigorous training to learn how to troubleshoot the aircraft I was assigned to work on and how to keep myself alive.

Then, one night, while I was asleep, I was abruptly awakened by a series of ear-splitting explosions. My first thought was that we were being bombed by our enemies. Instead, we were being alerted to man our battle stations to fight a fire that had erupted on the flight deck. It was everybody's job to fight a fire aboard the ship. If the ship were not saved, we would all surely die at sea. No sooner than I made it to the flight deck, I saw aircrafts exploding and panicked men everywhere. Some were on fire and others were jumping off the side of the ship that was ninety feet about sea level, to their imminent deaths.

That night, I saw some of the bravest acts of duty I had ever witnessed, as men risked their lives to save their brothers. We fought that fire all night and, when the smoke finally settled and the sun rose on the aftermath, there was nothing but signs of unspeakable destruction.

We lost twelve men and eight fighter jets that night. As we all sat upon the deck, exhausted, a solemn of quietness blanketed the ship throughout the day that followed. That catastrophic event seemed so surreal that I found myself in a state of shock, trying to comprehend what I had just experienced. It was then I came to the stark realization that I was expendable. Simply put, I was nothing more than a pawn in the upcoming war in which we were about to engage.

While I was overseas, my cousin, Monie, would occasionally send me huge care packages containing all kinds of goodies and homemade treats. With my bounty of goods, I would break bread with my brothers in my shop and ask everyone to thank God for Monie.

Lori would write me quite often. I even had a photo of her that I had placed on our "sweetheart board," and then would brag about her being the most beautiful young lady on the entire board.

At every country's port, where we were allowed to enter, we would be granted liberty, and I would call my mom. No matter what time it was stateside, she would always answer.

I was having the time of my young life and felt like a fictional character created in an adventure novel.

Although there were no American laws that governed us overseas, we were bound by those of the military. When given liberty, I worked hard and played even harder. At eighteen, I learned to drink, fight, and cuss like a sailor.

Thailand, Singapore, the Philippines, and Hong Kong were just a few of the western Pacific countries I was blessed to enter. Even though I really enjoyed the exotic nuances of the cultures and its people, I quickly recognized just how blessed I was to be a citizen of the United States.

While the severely impoverished Third World countries created mystical and sensual feelings, there was no denying the fact that we, Americans, took for granted the modern amenities we had in abundance at home.

On returning to the states, the first thing I did when my feet touched our soil was kiss the ground on which I stood and thanked God for America. Even though I was then stationed in California, there was just 'no place like home.'

At my new station, I met a brother by the name of Zach, who we called "Sad Cat." From South Central Los

Angeles, he had made it to our squadron, by way of a football injury in college that left him no longer able to play.

"Sad Cat" and I morphed into best friends at once. As a member of the Crips, one of Los Angeles' most prominent and notorious street gangs, "Sad Cat" had a lot of influence on me. After working hours, we drank heavily and repeatedly got into fights; marking our territory everywhere we went.

Eventually, I flew Lori out to see me. We had already made plans to be secretly married as soon as she arrived. We had a very small and sweet ceremony at a beautiful park in Fresno, and we basked in the reality that we finally were united as husband and wife.

The Navy gave us a house on base but, before we could officially begin our lives together, Lori had to go back to Rockford to gather her belongings and to get her son, DeMarco, who had been born into a previous relationship. Around the same time, Stephanie, the mother of my daughter, Ceara, had agreed to let her also come out to California to live with us and go to school. Sadly, though, Steph's plans fell through and Ceara was unable to join us.

While Lori was temporarily in Rockford to handle her business, I met a young lady named Chikena, on the flight line, while working at an air show. Chikena was in the Navy and, originally, hailed from Syracuse, New York.

Chikena, who I called "Kena," was really a nice girl, who reminded me of Serena Williams. As Chikena and I became more comfortable with each other, she and I ended up spending the weekend in my room at the barracks. But, with Lori due to return in two weeks from Rockford, Kena and I had to put an end to our short, passion-filled affair. I really like Kena, but the bottom line was... Lori was my wife.

After those two weeks passed, Lori and DeMarco returned to the base to move into our new home. Although we had sparse furnishings in our new house, we did have one another.

While I worked eight-hour shifts, Lori was a "stay-at-home mom." And, when it came to friends, we only had a couple that we could kick it with. Nevertheless, our three-bedroom home and love for one another was more than enough for us.

With Lori home, I now had to come up with a lie to tell Chikena, to make a clean break from an affair that we never should have allowed to happen. I concocted a story, sadly informing Kena that I had a death in my immediate family, and that I was being discharged from the Navy, so that I could be of help to my family. I believed that excuse would be valid enough to make me disappear from her life forever.

But as I said before; things change. About four or five months later, after a long day of work, Lori woke me up from a sound nap to tell me that a woman was on the phone, saying she was pregnant by me. The woman even went as far as relaying the message through Lori that, if I didn't get up and talk to her, there would be trouble like I had never known.

At first, I really thought I was dreaming but, after Lori refused to leave and continued trying to hand me the phone, I knew, right away, that the woman on the end of the other line could only be Kena.

I got up, grabbed the phone and, before I could barely say hello, Kena started railing about being pregnant, and she wanted me to be held accountable. I will admit that Kena and I did fall in love during those couple of weeks we spent together but now, she was expecting the impossible. She wanted me by her side and didn't care that Lori was my wife.

What made this entire situation more terrible than I could have imagined was the fact that Lori was also pregnant. She was expecting a baby that both she and I had planned for, shortly after she returned from Rockford. To make a long story short, everything that could have possibly hit the fan that day most certainly did. Lori was beyond hysterical, and there was absolutely nothing I could say that could begin to explain how much I had messed up.

Just as you probably imagine, our lives began to unravel right before our eyes. Lori quickly gave me an ultimatum; either forget about Chikena and the child that she was carrying, or she would leave me and move back to Rockford to live with her parents.

I found myself in quite a conundrum over having to choose between my wife and unborn child or abandoning Chikena and the baby she had conceived with me.

I chose not to abandon one nor to raise one without the other, so Lori left. While she and I remained legally married, the idea of being so close to the source that had destroyed everything we had dreamed of, was far more than Lori was willing to accept.

Not long, after Lori moved back to Rockford, Kena moved in with me. That's when I began living a dual life, promising, and telling Lori and Kena the same story that I would have a limited relationship with the other. As I struggled desperately, trying to deal with a very messy and tenuous situation, my drinking escalated to an all-time high.

Chikena and I grew closer together, but I was not any more loyal to her than I was to Lori. After a while, when Kena found out that I was cheating on her, she did her best to put up with me because, after all, she loved me and was having our child.

What everything boiled down to was that I had chosen Kena over Lori. I had made a big decision and gave up a lot to be with a woman I barely knew. From that point on, I believe that made all the difference in how she dealt with me.

On February 1, 1990, Chikena's and my son, Stephon was born. I had wanted Chikena to name him Stephen Troy, Jr., but she told me, 'One of you in the world is enough.' Nevertheless, I was extremely proud to have a son.

Then, nineteen days later, February 20, Lori gave birth to our son, Julian, in Rockford. Prior to Julian's birth, Lori had called me to let me know she was having some pregnancy complications, and she wanted me to come home. So, I went to my command staff to seek permission to leave, but my request was denied. So, without much thought, I left in the middle of the night and drove thirty-six hours alone, from California to Illinois, to be by Lori's side.

Technically, because I had abandoned my military duty without permission, I was considered AWOL (Absent Without Leave), and in serious trouble with "Uncle Sam." The FBI was sent to my parents' home, looking for me, but my mom refused to give me up. There was also no trace of the vehicle I had driven because I had hidden it. ·

I was happy to see that Julian had been born healthy, and that Lori was recovering well. To be honest, it felt good being back with my wife again but, to my discredit, I continued to make a lot of empty promises to not only her, but to Chikena, as well.

Over the next several days, Lori, Julian and I stayed with my parents until I could figure out what my next move would be. Any hope that I might have had about things working out, between Lori and me, quickly changed when Lori caught me talking on the phone with Kena. Suddenly, the grim reality of our situation resurfaced.

After being in Rockford for nearly two weeks, I decided to return to California to turn myself in, and to be with Kena and Stephon. And so, she and I lived together, working different shifts so we could share equal co-parenting responsibilities for Stephon.

I loved both women, and the two sons we shared together were a part of me that I cherished. Stephon and Julian were my seed, and I would do anything to protect and nourish them both.

One day, unexpectedly, when I returned to the apartment, I walked in the door to find it empty and a note next to a blanket and pillow lying on the floor. The note was from Kena informing me that she and Stephon had left California. Simultaneously, I had lost both women and children, and everything we had shared together was gone.

My life had spiraled out of control, and I still had to go and face the music with the Navy for taking an unauthorized leave. When I finally stood before my military officers, their punishment came swiftly. I was sentenced to ninety days in Treasure Island Federal Prison, located between the Golden Gate Bridge and Alcatraz, off the Bay of San Francisco, California.

As soon as my sentence ended, I was court-martialed by the Admiral of the Pacific Fleet, who told me that 'there was no room for people like me in his Navy.' As I was being processed out of the Navy, the Admiral basically called me the 'N-word' and said, 'good luck.' The Navy then stripped me of all my trainings, accommodations, certificates, and awards.

Depleted emotionally and physically, I returned home to Rockford, hoping to start all over again. Years passed before I heard from Chikena or saw Stephon, or even found out where they had gone. Now that everything and everyone in my life had been displaced, the reality of it all became very clear; these are the things that change "boys to men."

Chapter 4

I Got the Hook-Up

Now that I was, once again, back to Rockford with mom and dad, I managed to find a job at a small tire shop, re-treading semi-truck tires. I was the only black employee and, no sooner than Christmas rolled around, I was laid off and replaced by my boss's best friend; someone they had used me to train, so he could take my job.

Finding myself in economic straits, I was offered an opportunity to join a gang and sell cocaine. Finally, for the first time in my life, I had what I always wanted; street credibility, money, women, and a group of brothers who I believed would do any and everything for me.

Before long, I was partially responsible for the drugs in possession, and I had more money than I had ever seen in my life. Being ignorant to the severity of punishment, if encountered by the law, left me with a grandiose feeling. I felt like I was God of my world and that I needed nothing or no one ever again. I even remember telling my mother, one day, 'I will never work for the white man again.'

Like most young, ignorant people, I frivolously spent money on clothes, jewelry, women, and the fast life. With an endless, unaccountable supply of drugs and money, I began to experiment, diving deeper and deeper into a world that was strictly taboo. Then, one night, I broke the golden rule of the drug business; 'Don't get high on your own supply!'

With no shame, I vividly recanted my first use. Softly and dreamingly, I stated, 'that is what I've been looking for all of my life.' On a time-elapsed camera slowly unfolding in my mind, I vividly saw a meadow filled with countless rows of beautiful wildflowers of every imaginable color. As the flowers bathed themselves in the sun's golden rays on a perfect summer day, all my worries and troubles were gently lifted away, and I was left in this magnificent paradise to be untouched and free from everything and everybody.

That experience was one I would pay for with my life as I tried, time and time again, to relive the moment. A wise man once told me, 'Drugs will take you further than you're willing to go and keep you longer than you're willing to stay.'

When my daily activities were done, I continued to use nightly, in secret, with a friend and a family member. I had come to believe that the drugs were free since they were coming from an endless supply. The fact that they were never missed or had to be replaced didn't help; still, my situation was spiraling out of control.

I never once contemplated the irony that drugs would prove to put a priceless bounty on their own fruitfulness. A baffling and cunning trick used by the devil is to slowly allow me to trade in my identity for something I falsely believed I was so intelligent over and thought I could get away with.

Unknowingly, after I lost my position within the gang, I developed a serious drug habit that still had to be paid for; except, now, the money would have to come from my own resources. Cocaine is said to be a 'rich man's high,' because it is short-lived and needs to be replaced perpetually to continue to fulfill the sensation it gives.

Not long after the start of my drug use, my grand-mother, MaDear, became ill and passed away. This was, undisputedly, the worst thing that had ever happened to our family. It was like the master link to a chain had been removed, and the chain no longer functioned and was no good for anything at all.

My heart felt like it had literally been ripped out of my body, and my chest was left with nothing but a black, empty hole. I wanted to be neither here nor there and wanted nothing more out of life than to escape the reality in which I was being forced to live.

I moved into my grandmother's basement with my cousins and set up an environment that was equivalent to a domestic crack house hidden in plain sight. We called it the "Dog Pound."

It was a family affair, because everyone who resided in the basement were strung out on plentiful supplies of cocaine, marijuana and alcohol that were regularly delivered through a revolving door. In the process, I found no reprieve in this situation and only learned more cunning ways to lie, scheme and cheat my way into getting more money and drugs.

One night, while I was at a high school basketball game, I met a girl named Rachael. Though she was only sixteen, I began creeping around with her and found myself in another "should not have been" love affair.

Rachael was sweet, intelligent, reserved and very mature for her age. But, when she got pregnant well into our relationship, I had to go and meet her parents. Her mother was a kind and understanding woman, but her dad was another story altogether. He was emphatic about not wanting me with his daughter, and it didn't matter what I said or promised. His stance did not change. It was only after Rachael threatened to never speak to her father again or to have anything to ever do with him, that he eased up.

Rachael gave birth to our daughter, Ashlee, the day after Christmas in 1992. Ashlee's birth was a difficult delivery, and she was born with a few physical ailments that had her admitted in Pediatric Intensive Care. Ashlee proved to be a strong and determined baby as she fought her way to good health, and she was finally able to go home.

I was twenty-two years old with four children and four "Baby Mommas." And no matter how much I wanted and tried to assert myself as a father, the drugs proved to be stronger and kept me disabled. During this time, I was not a functioning addict at all. The ups and downs of an acute cocaine addiction left me all but crippled. My relationships at home with my immediate family had all but dissipated, and I was forced to find different ways to come up with an income to support my daily drug habit. After long, as might be expected, I couldn't hold a job or keep a promise, so stealing became my next best option.

I made an unsuccessful attempt to relocate to Atlanta, Georgia with my Uncle Sammy, only to end up homeless and in search for the nearest Red Cross Shelter.

With everything I owned being carried in a Navy Sea bag, it was by fate that I ran into my Auntie Candee, who was a relative of my biological father. By chance, when Auntie Candee noticed me walking past her Eastside apartment, she quickly ran to the door and yelled, 'Stevie!' The rest was history.

Unknown to me at the time, Auntie Candee was pimpin' and selling drugs to support her lifestyle and serious cocaine habit. She schooled me on the games of the streets, one step at a time. She, herself, had been an addict all her life, so she understood the importance of me learning how to survive a life on the dangerous streets of Atlanta.

Aunt Candee took me under her wing and introduced me to the big-time players and women who were constantly around her. She never left me behind and always loved and cared for me in a way that no one else could or would at that time. Auntie Candee promised not to make a poor hustler out of me and, when I messed up, she made sure I learned what I did wrong, until I didn't make the same mistake again.

Auntie might have been small in stature, but she was big in personality and character. She also was ill with H.I.V. and really needed me to look out for her, just as much as I needed her.

The Eastside of town, where Auntie Candee and I lived was notorious for drugs, crime, and prostitution. It was also quite a remarkable market for an underground world, particularly, in a city with a reasonably average population. It was like being in a different dimension or time zone, as I found myself amazed, captivated, and intertwined in the land of 'The Eastside' and becoming one with it.

Living day to day and just enough for the city was the life for me. I had no one to answer to; I was high all the time, and I was enjoying the street life like there was no tomorrow. Subsequently, I changed my name to 'B.D. (Black Disciple) Steve' from the Eastside streets.

As I continued to prosper, I saw it as a spiritual blessing, but not from the loving God I knew. I had been blessed, by the dark side, to have everything I would always need. Those blessings also ensured I would remain divided from my family, subtracted from the world, and sentenced to an imminent death, if not saved or rescued in time.

Only God in Heaven could save me now. I had sold my soul to the devil, and I had voluntarily and, at the same time, involuntarily traded in everything that mattered for the life I now so vainly glorified.

The saddest part about my downfall was the worst was yet to come.

Chapter 5

The Wheat and the Tares

There is an old parable in the New Testament of the Holy Bible, where workers were hired to go into the field to separate the wheat from the tares.

The wheat, which was productive for food and life, was to be removed from the tares, which were a cancer to the wheat. It was basically a weed that had to be uprooted so that the wheat could achieve its purpose and be fruitful.

The problem, then and even to this day, is that the wheat and the tares look alike. It takes a trained eye and expertise to ensure that one is not confused with the other. There is a great chance that the good can be mistakenly discarded, instead of the bad.

There are some who have been blessed with the spiritual gift of discernment. I have always had this gift; being able to easily discern the real from an imposter, good from bad, and ultimately the overplay for the underplay.

In life, you always have those that are superior in using one person to take the blame for something in which they aren't responsible. Oftentimes, this can lead to the "fall guy" being severely injured or even killed.

I was taught, while "life is a cold-blooded game," it is often fair. On the other hand, it can be a "dog-eat-dog world," where only the strong and most cunning survive. In this new life that I had fallen into, not only do you have to worry about the drugs killing you, but the stick-up man, opposition gangs and crooked cops are just as worrisome.

I have often found myself on the wrong end of this equation; easily becoming the victim because of the volume of criminal activity in which I allowed myself to be involved. Because of the reputation I had developed, I was viewed as a dangerous threat on the streets.

My philosophy was… 'I will be the last man standing at-all-times, and in every circumstance, no matter what.' I lived by the internal decision that I was going to hurt you before you could hurt me. Being allied with most of the heavy hitters on the land also kept about seventy-five percent of those questioning themselves about challenging me or not. Most of the time, they chose the latter.

It's the same everywhere you go, and I took my gift with me from city to city, and town to town across the Midwest. The downside was, the bigger the market was, the greater the chances were that something bad could happen to you. Yet, the upside was that the greater the risk was, the greater the reward would be.

Chicago, Illinois has gained a well-earned reputation as 'Gangland, U.S.A.,' and it's where I found myself on its treacherous streets, all alone, lost, and hungry.

The same hunger that pained me from lack of nutrition was shifted to the hunger that always leads me to find a means of making a quick buck, finding a haven of safety, and someone down with me to share my joy and pain.

In an emergency, I sought information from a fire station and was directed to an overnight shelter on Chicago's north side. It was nothing more than an open gym with mats on the floor and an issued sheet that did little to keep me warm.

Upon awakening the next morning, I rolled over to see Cedric, a young brother I knew from a Rehab program in the city. He welcomed me with open arms and invited me to spend the day with him. It was check day, or as it was mostly referred to, "Lord, Have Mercy Day," and we headed to the nearest currency exchange, where hundreds of individuals patiently waited in line to receive their monthly benefits.

Cedric was part of a local gang and introduced me to his guys. As a guest on their land, we became good friends, and he taught me how to navigate the land and the big city way of getting down.

In the morning, I hustled at a moving company, and at night I "jacked," strong-armed or robbed unsuspecting victims. The hits were flawless, as the monstrous size of Chicago enabled us to hit the L-Train and be thirty blocks away in any direction within minutes.

I started copping my drugs from the infamous Cabrini Green Housing Projects. I would go through a gauntlet of changes to get right, then I'd go in the back of an open-air drug market, back on familiar territory to get high, and redirect their traffic to buy drugs from me right behind their backs.

I was playing an incredibly dangerous game, but the reward and ease of maintaining my habit was more than worth it to me. I was getting better quality and larger amounts of drugs from Cabrini Green at a lower price. With those odds, I couldn't lose.

One day, Cedric, and I had been messing around and getting high. With no regard for our well-being, we found ourselves in a familiar situation; we had no money, no food and nowhere to go.

My first suggestion was to go and steal something to eat, which wasn't hard to do at all. But Cedric stopped me and challenged me to ask my God, that I was always bragging so much about, to feed us. Cedric didn't really believe in anything, and he most assuredly didn't believe in Jesus. So, I thought of Elijah, a prophet in the Old Testament, and how he dug a trench and prayed to God for rain from heaven. Cedric's challenge was for non-believers. As we continued to walk, I silently prayed to the Lord Jesus to forgive me and my friend and to, please, somehow, provide us with something to eat.

No sooner than we reached the end of the block and turned the corner and began walking up the other side, about halfway up the next block, I saw a McDonald's bag neatly folded, sitting in the middle of the sidewalk. I picked up the bag and opened it. Inside were two 'Big Macs' and two orders of fries; all neatly wrapped, untouched, free from insects and still warm.

Right there on that city block, I praised God and thanked him for the small miracle he had provided for us. I don't believe we said another word to one another that night. The awesome power of God had manifested itself right in our presence.

After nearly a year in Chicago, living from hand to mouth, I called home and begged my mother for a bus ticket home. Confessing to her that my activities, lifestyle, and Chicago were going to land me in prison or an early grave, she came through, as always. Before our call ended, my mother told me that she was giving me "one shot" to get home. She let me know, in no uncertain terms, that when I made my decision, I needed to make it wisely.

I made my way to O'Hare Airport and caught the Rockford-O'Hare bus back home the same day. Waiting to pick me up at the bus station was my ex-wife, Lori, and Julian, who dropped me off at mom and dad's.

It was such a relief to be back home and safe again. It was as if I had stepped out of a dreadful night into a golden day. After a couple of days' rest, I returned to the land, Rockford's East side and picked up right where I left off.

It was there, where I ran into Melissa, a transient from Peoria. I quickly finessed my way into her life and, before long, I had turned her apartment into a "trap" and soon caught my first serious criminal offense. The police conducted a raid, and I was caught with over twelve grams of crack cocaine, bagged and in the process of being distributed. I was charged with manufacturing and delivering a controlled substance and housed in the Winnebago County jail on a five hundred thousand dollars bond.

After a several months of litigation, I was offered a first-time offender's program. The charge had been lowered to "possession," with a couple of years of intense probation included. Of course, I took the deal and headed back to the block, where I was rewarded with gifts and much love from the gang. They set me up with enough resources to pick me up and get me started again.

At this time, we were trappin' at a flea-bag hotel, named the Grand Hotel. It was a twenty-four hour, seven days a week entity that was open for drugs, crime, and prostitution. The Grand was an underground landmark that was doing some serious numbers. The police were afraid to intercede on our perpetual affairs, as it was, a stronghold for gangs and cliques that resided there. It had the aura of being one of the great wonders of the world. Money seemingly and almost literally fell from the sky. The Grand is where I also became cool with a brother by the name of "Detroit Red." He was a transplant on the land, from the "Motor City."

Once you're accepted on the block, you're treated like family; that is, until something happens that changes everything. Take for instance, the night Red's girl ran off with all his drugs and money.

I had been riding around in a stolen van for most of the summer and had been on about a twenty-five days' crack binge without any sleep. I decided to help Red out because I knew once he was straight again, he would forever be loyal to me. So, we took off, in a stolen van, to go on a shoplifting spree, and we found ourselves on the outskirts of the town.

While heading back to our connection to re-up, I fell asleep at the wheel. Traveling at about forty-five m.p.h., the van drifted off into incoming traffic and hit a flatbed, semi-truck head on. When I regained consciousness, Red was smashed face first into the windshield, and the truck's fuel line had broken, spraying diesel fuel all over the van.

Good Samaritans from everywhere converged on the scene and rescued me and Red. We were placed in separate ambulances and taken to the nearest hospital. Because the van had been reported stolen, I gave the paramedics and police a fake name when they asked for my identity.

Out of nowhere, my Aunt Lois, who I had probably not seen in over a year, ran up to the ambulance screaming my name. When I awoke, I was handcuffed to a gurney in the hospital's Emergency Room. And although, I hadn't been home or called my parents in six months or more, my mom and dad were sitting at my side.

The doctor examined a couple of my glass infused lacerations but, because I had become irate and was in a drug driven haze, I refused to allow him to proceed any further in treating or stitching up my injuries.

Meanwhile, although we didn't know it at the time, word had moved quite swiftly at the county jail that Red had died from his injuries. Upon my release from the emergency room, my mom told me to go and check on Red. When I eventually made it to the land, I was glad to see that, aside from suffering some severe facial lacerations, 'Detroit Red' was alive and well, and just as glad to see me, too.

We had both survived a near death experience. It was a miracle that we were alive, but instead of thanking God, Red hit me with a large supply of cocaine, and I continued on my merry way.

By 1995, I totally switched gears. I went from "robbin' and stealing" to "pimpin' and selling dope."

There were so many young girls lost and turned out on the track. For their well-being, they chose brothers who could make sure they were safe, clothed, fed, had a roof of any kind over their heads, and didn't mind being their "Daddy."

I could use my name and clout to get deals on drugs that others couldn't, which also proved to be an advantage in having a girl or two who was always willing to be under my administration.

Being smooth with the tongue, blessed in the game and a true hustler, I made a seamless transition to my newfound occupation.

'Anything goes when it comes to hoes, cause pimpin' ain't easy!'

Pimpin' turned out to be a mental game that required a little more than strength and muscle. I quickly realized that it was going to take a few lessons and a lot of learning to master this side of the game.

Chapter 6

Torn Between Two Lovers

One day, when Pastor Wolfe suggested that I enter a faith-based treatment program, I only did it because he recommended it and not because I wanted to quit getting high.

After a couple of months, I ran into an old girlfriend's daughter, Keri Ann, who was quite surprised to see me clean and sober. She quickly called her mom, Kathy, who couldn't wait to see me.

Kathy, a white woman from a rural town in Illinois, was seventeen years older than me. Once a former addict, she had quit using, years ago, gotten her life back on track, and had moved into a nice apartment.

After finally seeing Kathy, we slowly resumed our relationship, and it proved to be better than it was when we last ended it. When she welcomed me into her home, I left the treatment program and moved in with her. It meant I wouldn't have to be on the streets any longer. All she asked was that I not steal anything from her home and to be there when she returned from work. I could basically do as I pleased, at her expense.

Kathy's invitation to me was a convenient proposal to which I quickly adapted.

She cooked, cleaned, loved me down, bought me gifts and, occasionally, did things for my children.' Because Kathy was so good to me, most began to view me as her "boy-toy" or "trophy" and, unwittingly, she eventually started to enable me in my addiction.

After a while, her daughter, Keri Ann, began showing resentment because she didn't like the idea that things were working out so good for me and that I had become "king of the castle."

Then, suddenly, one morning while her mother was at work, Keri Ann began parading around the apartment with little to nothing on. It appeared she was either attempting to seduce me or trying me to see how I would react. I chose to respond by staying in the bedroom all day, while Kathy was at work, and only came out to use the bathroom or to hit the fridge. After a couple of weeks, I eventually told Kathy about Keri Ann's behavior and asked her to speak to her about dressing more appropriately around me.

Now don't get me wrong, Keri Ann was attractive, and we were about the same age. And, just like most men love a hot juicy fling every now and then, I had played the entire scenario out in my head and decided against making any advances toward Keri Ann. Afterall, she was my woman's daughter, and I just couldn't cross that line. Besides, I knew if I did, she would tell her mom, and I would lose Kathy.

As it turned out, most of the men Kathy dated, at one time or another, had made a move on Keri Ann and had even sexually assaulted her. So, when I chose to ignore her advances, though Keri Ann was surprised, she praised me for my integrity, and finally accepted me as part of her family. Over the years as we grew closer and accepted each other with unconditional love, Kathy and Keri Ann became my immediate family.

In Kathy's attempt to protect me from the streets, she allowed me to use at home and, when the temptation of watching me proved too great of an enticement, she began sporadically getting high with me during her days off. I don't want to minimize Kathy's drug abuse, but she had tremendous will power. She managed to function quite normally and maintained a grip on all her responsibilities, including me.

Because Kathy knew I had a passion for cooking and my reputed culinary skills were known around the town's restaurant industry, it didn't take much for her to convince me that I should put my skills to use at some of the nice restaurants in the vicinity of where we lived.

What made this venture ideal was the fact that I could basically choose where I wanted to work, and I could name my hourly wage.

Almost immediately, I became an asset to any kitchen that utilized my skills, and I could be trusted and depended upon, no matter where I worked, to ensure that the owner's operation ran smoothly, efficiently, and productively. As a result, to a certain extent, I became successful.

Realistically, however, no matter how successful one might become, if untreated and unresolved problems, like my addictions to drugs and the game, continued to exist, there was absolutely no way I could ever take full control of my life. My irregular attendance and not showing up when

I was needed most, became my downfall, and prevented me from holding down a long-term job.

In most of the spots I worked, I began selling drugs and, when it came down to the people I associated with, my poor discretion usually found me in the company of questionable and undesirable acquaintances. Randomly, I'd drift from the streets to back home, until I finally ended up back in another faith-based treatment program out of town.

Pacific Garden Mission, a homeless shelter in downtown Chicago, had an intense program, and it was recommended to me by Pastor Wolfe, who was the head of a program in Rockford.

Once I arrived in Chicago, I immediately began immersing myself in the Word of God. I became a prayer warrior and formed a spiritual warfare team with a couple of the other brothers who were also there for treatment. We casted out demons and constantly stayed on alert for the enemy who was, without a doubt, always on the attack.

Amazingly, one morning, we were approached by a young man that none of us recognized as a guest or transient who had come through or frequented the Mission before. With so many different souls and men, from some of the city's harshest conditions, constantly coming through the Mission's doors, the environment often felt like a cesspool for demons.

On that day, the man asked if we would allow him to assist us in our quest to patrol, guard and stand watch against the evil spirits that dwelled in the building. And, even though, none of us had ever spoken to this gentleman before, he seemed all too familiar with our tactics, outline, and game plan against the enemy.

We found the man to be very effective and, for a few short days, he took the lead in our defense. His demeanor was stoic, and he was well educated and versed in the Word.

After a week, the mysterious man suddenly disappeared, and we never saw him again. As I thought about how he had appeared "from out of the blue," I truly came to believe that he was an administering angel who had come down from Heaven to entertain, bless and assist us.

At this point, God was so real in my life that I found myself walking in the Spirit, as I consciously denied my flesh.

It was then a powerful Baptist preacher named Pastor Mims, who was the head of the program and the very notarized men's choir at the Mission, appointed me to oversee one of the shelter's floors, where I stood watch over the guests and transients who visited every night.

One evening, while I was reading and studying the Book of Isaiah, the words suddenly began jumping off the page at me. The passage that I was reading took on a new form and turned into a motion picture in my mind and spirit. That was the moment the Bible turned into "The Living Word of God" for me.

Not long after, I received a letter in the mail. As I read the letterhead, the name didn't ring a bell. The letter had come from a young lady named Melanie, who said that she was struggling with an issue over who the father of her unborn child was. She was early on in her pregnancy and was very embarrassed about the ordeal in which she found herself.

Melanie revealed that she had met me one evening, while volunteering at a program, of which her father was on the Board of Directors. She reached out to her parents about me and learned of my whereabouts and began seeking some spiritual guidance and someone to confide in over her dilemma. After several exchanges of correspondence,

Melanie and I developed a mutual and respectful attraction for one another.

When my Aunt Candee, who had raised me in the streets of Atlanta, passed away in Rockford after a long bout with H.I.V. and AIDS, I asked Melanie if she would take me to the funeral. Without hesitation, she agreed.

At the service, I was stunned that, out of all Aunt Candee's many friends, there wasn't one willing to say a final word over her, so I stood up and went to the podium. I spoke about the two thieves, Dismas (the good thief) and Gestas (the bad thief), who were crucified on crosses to the right and left of Jesus. Gestas, refusing to believe that Jesus was the Messiah, taunted and rebuked Jesus, along with the crowd. Meanwhile, Dismas, who had accepted that Jesus was indeed the Son of God, offered a plea of mercy as he hung dying, which allowed him to enter paradise with Jesus on the day that they both died.

I was told that as Aunt Candee laid on her deathbed, she accepted Jesus. The message I wanted to impart to the unruly crowd was that it was never too late to be saved. And even though I knew, in my heart, my aunt was no longer suffering, losing her hurt and saddened me, more than I can say. Her death made me feel like another piece of me had been thrown away, just as it had when my beloved MaDear passed away.

Meanwhile, my relationship with Melanie evolved into one of the most intimate and love-filled relationship I had ever been in. Mel and I were extremely compatible and quite possibly soul mates.

During the summer, Chikena allowed my son, Stephon, to visit. In order to spend every moment with him, I left the program in Chicago and moved back in with mom. After having been away from Stephon for so long, it felt so good to have him back in my presence. Chikena had done a great job in raising him, and he was a joy to be around!

I managed to get Stephon and his brother, Julian, together as many times as possible. It was always my prayer that they would grow up and be as close as my brothers and I were. Their relationship always seemed special to me, because their age difference was only nineteen days; just as my sister, Treece, and I are the same age.

Melanie, her father, Rick, and her grandmother, "Grandma Betty," were ecstatic over Stephon. They spoiled him with gifts and plenty of love.

Mel and her family were the ones who made me finally realize that not all white people were bad. They all had hearts of gold and were very sound Christians, who didn't see life's issues in terms of black or white; only right and wrong.

As summer rolled around, it would be a summer to remember. It would also be the last time I laid eyes on Stephon or even spoke to him. While I can't put my finger on why that happened, I do know that our adversary is always lurking around every crook and cranny, seeking whomever and whatever it can devour.

Right before Stephon returned home to New York, I started using again and initiated the roller coaster ride that had become all too familiar once again.

Then, on a beautiful summer day, Melanie, some friends, and I were on our way to a picnic, when we came upon an accident in the same direction we were going. Proceeding on to our destination, we didn't think anything else about it. But, when we eventually returned home and were pulling into the driveway, my dad came running down the driveway, shouting, "Arthur Jr. is dead!"

Arthur was a very close cousin of mine that I grew up with and affectionately called "New Jack." Arthur had only been a block away from home when he was involved in a motorcycle accident. It was a tragic event that devastated the whole family. I was in mourning and at my lowest state, when I called Kathy, who also had been close to "New Jack."

Kathy and Keri Ann offered me comfort as I agonized over the loss of my cousin. While I didn't realize it at the time, this period would find me trapped in a revolving door between the lives of Kathy and Melanie. My inability to commit to a faithful relationship with either one made me feel like I was on a "seesaw" that never stopped going up or down.

Kathy and Melanie's tug-of-war was in full effect as they fought for my attention and affection. With both holding equal parts of my heart and desire, we became entangled in a messy love triangle that seemed to never end. When the smoke finally ended, Mel and I got an apartment together. I got a job, cooking at a steakhouse and found a new edition to my struggle as a functional addict.

In the interim, Melanie finally had her daughter, and we named her Trinity. I wanted Trinity to be my daughter, so bad. By her being bi-racial, people automatically assumed that I was her father anyway.

Spending time with my children was important to me, so I tried to pick up my daughter, Ceara, every weekend. Stephanie didn't have any problem with me being in Ceara's life, and she also seemed to understand that I was doing the best I could for her.

Occasionally, I'd get Julian and Ashlee and would spend time with them, doing all kinds of fun things together and taking road trips out of town as a family. Melanie loved and accepted my children, and she understood how important they were to me.

Then, one day, unexpectedly, I got a phone call from Rachael asking if I would take care of Ashlee for a while. I talked to Mel about it, and we prepared to move Ashlee in with us.

On the afternoon I was scheduled pick my daughter up, we got a message on the answering machine that Ashlee, who had been left unattended, had been severely burned while trying to cook on the stove. Ashlee had been taken to the Emergency Room, in serious condition, with burns over a large portion of her body. While my baby laid in the Pediatric Burn Unit for some time, I prayed endlessly, asking God to take the pain away from Ashlee, and to give it to me. This moment was the most helpless I had ever felt, because I knew there was absolutely nothing that I could do to make my baby girl better. We all spent days and nights, around the clock, with Ashlee until she got better.

When I finally proposed to Melanie, our engagement to be married was doomed from the start. It quickly derailed, never happened and, truth be told, it was because I just could never seem to hold it together.

At an apex of my addiction, I wound up in prison for a short bid, and then returned to the streets. I now had the qualification of a "hardened convict" to add to my resume.'

> Melanie and Kathy were both still
> around, but I chose the streets over them.
> Subsequently, Melanie moved out of state,
> and Kathy moved out of town.

Chapter 7

PIMP

I was chosen by a hardcore hooker from the land, who was giving me three hundred to a thousand dollars a day. My habit had escalated to an all-time high, and the hooks of my addiction dug deeper and deeper into my soul.

I picked up two or three different girls, and we began pulling off armed robberies which I learned was a faster way of getting "quick money" than selling drugs. That didn't last very long, because my reckless behavior led me to being quickly apprehended by the law and sent back to prison.

During this incarceration, I was diagnosed with several mental health challenges which included anxiety disorder. I was schizoaffective and, also, suffered from P.T.S.D. (Post Traumatic Stress Disorder) as a result of the horrific flight deck fire that occurred while I was aboard the aircraft carrier during my time in the Navy.

I quickly became one of the prison's guinea pigs as their medical staff experimented with various psychotropic medications. Over time, as so many others do, I developed a dependence on them.

Once I was finally released from prison, nothing really changed. I had only been back on the streets for a very short time before I found myself back in the custody of Illinois' fine Department of Corrections. This time I was charged with commercial burglary, on top of the two-armed robberies that were already on my record.

At this point in my life, I felt like I had traded in far too much, simply to leave the game without checking the big ticket, or sting, which would leave me satisfied for all I had been through. The truth of the matter was my addiction was insatiable.

I had gotten a call from my mom, telling me that one of my childhood friends, Kemra, had called, inquiring about me. Kemra was opening a restaurant in downtown Rockford, and she wanted to give me an opportunity to manage her kitchen. After thinking about it, I thought, I would give it a try, so I cleaned myself up and met with Kemra and her distributor at the restaurant.

At the time, I was seeing a girl, who was extremely jealous that I might be leaving my full-time occupation on the streets for a "real" job. She cried, whined, and made promises, hoping it would coerce me into deciding to stay in the streets. But, to my misfortune, for reasons still unknown to me, the job never came to fruition, and the vicious cycle of my addiction continued.

For the next few years, I stayed in dope houses, abandoned homes and one sleazy hotel after another. In the words of the mighty Temptations, without a doubt, this 'Poppa was a rolling stone, and wherever I laid my hat was my home!'

By then, the Rockford police were all too familiar with me. I was always under microscopic surveillance, and they even went as far as referring to me and my bottom-girl, Stacey, as "Bonnie and Clyde."

Now, Stacey was a gangsta, and she was down for just about any diabolical scheme that came to my mind. Heavy in our addictions and in one constant situation after another on the land, Stacey and I clung together like Siamese twins. The toxic love we had for one another was all we felt we had in our lives, and it made us feel like we weren't alone.

Time and time again, Stacey never hesitated to prove her unflinching loyalty to me. She was straightforward about how she felt about me, and I knew that, no matter what ever happened, she would always hold me down. In the truest sense, she was my "ride or die" partner and friend!

Then, once again, there was Melissa, the transient I had met in Peoria. Five years after I last saw her, Melissa hunted me down and showed me a photo of a little girl that she swore up and down was mine. But, after all that time, there was no way I could ever believe that child belonged to me. Still hoping to convince me that I, in fact, had fathered her child, Melissa, once again, held the photo up in front of my face, so I could have a better look.

Closely examining the photo, I had to admit that Melissa had not been mistaken; that little girl, whose name was Lasha, had eyes like mine. And, although Melissa had given her up at birth, Lasha's adoptive family blessed Melissa with the opportunity to remain a part of her life.

I didn't really know what to think. At this point in my life, I didn't want any more kids. I had enough problems trying to take care of myself, let alone becoming responsible for another seed. Melissa, on the other hand, was head over heels, infatuated and, hopelessly, in love with me that she refused to give up on me in my confusion to accept Lasha.

As time passed, I had a few brief encounters with Lasha. She turned out to be a beautiful little girl and, the more I looked at her, it occurred to me that she looked a lot like my mom. Unfortunately, my relationship with Lasha ended up being so estranged that I accepted the fact she was far better off being with her adoptive parents than me or Melissa.

Lasha will forever be a piece of me, and I pray that God will have the final say on how the future turns out between the two of us.

I never gave up my dream of, one day, hitting it big in the music industry. Seeing such a dream come to fruition could take me and Stacey off the streets and out of the clutches of our addictions.

Now, I was still a Christian in my heart and Stacey knew how I felt about God, even though she practiced witchcraft and was bi-sexual. During our darkest of times,

I often reassured Stacey that God would be there to help us endure every storm we faced.

Stacey had a dark past. She had been physically and mentally abused by her ex-husband, who also physically and sexually abused her three children. Sadly, she ultimately lost her children to the system, due to her fear of informing authorities about her ex-husband's offenses.

Stacey also told me that, at one point, she had been diagnosed with an acute stomach cancer. Though doctors had not been optimistic and didn't give her any hope of getting well, Stacey proved them wrong and survived.

When Stacey got pregnant, she carried our child to full term, only to give birth to a stillborn baby boy, with a full head of black hair. Stacey named our son, Steven Troy Hanserd, Jr., and her mother laid him to rest in an undisclosed location.

Once again, I had made another baby, and even though I never had the chance of sharing a life with him, I thank God that Steven did not have to be born into the world in which his mother and I had become entrapped.

There was no way that I could leave Stacey alone to die in the streets, so I tried all I could to change our self-defeating lifestyle. The truth was, however, how could I save someone else, if I had no possibility of saving myself? So, guess what happened? You would be right if you said I went back to the 'Big House,' and I never saw Stacey again.

Chapter 8

When You're All Alone

It's funny how, when the party is over, everyone goes their own way and forgets you ever existed. When fun, laughter, money, drugs, and women are readily available, an abundance of people are always standing by to reap the benefits. These are the same people who will go out of their way to convince you that they have your back, no matter what. And, while I never believe all the lies, smiles, and promises that are politically motivated when you're on top and life is good, most know, by now, that you should never take me for a fool.

The hardened pain of this reality comes when the lights go out and you're all alone. I've always been so blessed that God has always left an indestructible bridge between my mother and my aunts, Pat, and Laci. When there is no one or nowhere else to turn and the shifting sand, on which I have repeatedly laid my foundation, has collapsed, I can count on their support. And, while I have no doubt that the disappointment, I have caused is deeply embedded in their hearts, their love and unwavering support for me remain unconditional.

When it comes to being incarcerated, nothing is free. The Department of Corrections' outlandish price tags, whether tangible or intangible, come at exorbitant costs that include the separation from family and loved ones, loss of self-respect, self-esteem issues, depression, loss of hope, and self-defamation of character. The costliest of all, however, is the loss of one's freedom and precious time that can never be given back.

The privilege of having a television, clothing, personal hygiene products, food, and shoes, also prove to be quite costly. The penal system has deliberately devised profitable ways to ensure that you will pay for everything you need and, if you can't afford their costs, you will go without. They offer no perks nor freebies.

The prison system also understands the importance of an incarcerated individual's need to be reconciled through occasional visits with their families to remain connected and through regular phone communication to make out-rageously-priced, "by-the-minute" calls that are paid by the receiving party.

Like so many others, I am never prepared for nor able to afford how the system so brazenly and insensitively takes advantage of inmates without any accountability. Yet, time after time, somehow and some way, the Lord always provides me with all that I need.

Most of the time, I have something to share with someone who would love to be in my shoes. In fact, my grandmother would sometimes tell me, 'Stevie, if everyone put all their problems in a big bag and shook them up and picked one, when it became time for you to pick a problem, you'd be digging deep in the bag looking for your own.'

Being back in prison again, to face a ten-year sentence and having to endure the repeated pain of being locked up like a caged animal, forced me to face the fact that, if anything were to ever get better for me, I'd have to commit myself to some new life choices.

Then, one night as I slept in my cell during the wee hours of the morning, I was awakened by a voice so loud and clear, that it seemed as if another person had come into my cell; but I was alone.

The voice said 'Why don't you trust me? You have tried everything else. So, why don't you trust me?' God had come into my cell that night and offered me the opportunity to allow him to make my life right.

I sat up in my bed and said, "Alright, Lord, I will. Nothing else I have done has worked for me, so I'm going to put my trust in you."

Suddenly, every thought and desire I had about using drugs or being on the streets left me. The taste of cocaine and alcohol slowly faded from my memory and phantom taste buds. I started making a conscientious decision to begin praying, attending church services, and going to school.

A healing process had begun in my life, mind, and spirit. Positivity, hope, and inspiration returned to me after years of battling myself, my addiction and God.

Because I had always cut hair, ever since I was in the Navy and had been blessed to have the ability to do it well, I entered cosmetology school and began working on my license and certification. Academically, I flourished in class, as well as on the shop floor with an overall 3.6 grade point average, and I became a teacher's aide. By that time, I had eighty-one credits toward my Associates Degree in General Studies, when I only needed sixty. Carrying a 4.0 grade point average, I graduated with Honor Cum Laude, at the top of my class and, suddenly, life had taken on a whole new meaning for me. I felt brand new.

When I spoke to my mom, one day, she told me that my friend, Kemra, had asked about me, and she wanted to write to me. From what I knew, Kemra was going through a messy divorce. Knowing that as well, my mom suggested that I stay focused and concentrate on preparing to come home. But that night as I watched television, more than once, I thought, about Kemra. So, I prayed.

Now, I know this sounds crazy because I hadn't talked to or seen Kemra in ages, but there was something in my spirit that allowed me to continue feeling the way I did about her.

With about eighteen months left on my ten-year sentence, I kept my hand to the plow. Now, don't get me wrong, I didn't turn into an angel overnight. I was still involved in some extracurricular activities behind those prison walls. I was still gang affiliated, which is not that easy to denounce, and I was still nickel and dime hustling on the side to make ends meet.

So, you see, I still couldn't completely surrender by letting go of everything. I freed myself only of the things I wanted gone the most, and I handed them over to God. Everything else, I neatly tucked away in my back pocket and found some irrational reasoning to justify holding on to them. Besides, they were my personal secrets, and no one would ever know anything about them; that is, except me and God.

There had been so many days and long nights on the streets, that I wandered aimlessly throughout the land, with nowhere to go or no one to turn to. It was easy being mad at myself for making the same stupid decision again, for the "umpteenth" time to use drugs, hoping to convince myself that somehow the outcome would be different this time. But, at the end of the day, I'd end up slapping myself in the face with the harsh reality that here I am again, at the end of that cold, lonely road, facing another brick wall. Two choices laid before me - (1) I could kill myself, which I was slowly doing anyway, or (2) I could do an "about face" and go back the other way by finding the strength from somewhere deep within, to try again and to cope with the way things needed to be. It's such a tricky situation because, when the first opportunity presents itself for someone to use again, generally, it's off to the races they go.

All the while, they keep questioning if they were lying to yourself all along? Were they padding their feelings just to get through the pain of withdrawal and depression, until the next available episode to begin and initiate this continuous process all over again?

I began asking myself, "Am I addicted, or have I been affected?" Had I inherited some generational curse? After all, my biological father, William, and a host of other family members also struggled with addictions of their own, though none seemingly to the severity of mine.

When you're out in the world, caught up in the rat race of the dope game, you don't have time, nor the mindset to think about how or why you got to where you are. All that exist is the pressing need to ease the pain of it all, with whatever will help you escape all your problems by masking them with the elixir of the drugs and alcohol. It becomes your medicinal fix, prescribed by the enemy, to be administered dose after dose, while never fulfilling the promise of permanent relief.

My God had decided that the only way to gain my attention was to separate me from the world and rat race. He wanted to make sure that I could hear from Heaven and seek His face. To my credit, I had not been arrested but, once again, was rescued and saved from myself and the incredibly dangerous lifestyle I so egregiously craved.

I focused on my psychiatric issues, and with the help of my doctor, I began the arduous journey of getting off the psychotropic medications as well. I got honest and came to the terms that I was only using the meds, at this time, to substitute for the cocaine and alcohol. I had been using them as a crutch to escape my reality at night; the moment when everything always raced through my mind and tortured me.

I requested that all narcotic medication, of which I was prescribed, be switched to non-narcotic, then I slowly weaned myself off those. When my mind started to clear up, I physically and mentally began to feel better about myself.

I realized the battlefield of my turmoil was largely in my mind. I had been brainwashed by the streets and drugs.

After reading Roman 12:2 which says, 'Be ye transformed by the renewing of your mind,' I knew I needed to get back to some form of Steve that was acceptable not only to myself, but to society. I had to allow my brain to be washed again, but this time it needed to be cleansed by the blood of the Lamb!

Chapter 9

Never Give Up

Upon my release from prison in 2016, surprisingly, my mother asked if I would parole back home. She didn't want me back on the streets. What she wanted was to give me the most favorable opportunity to find the right path to my own success.

I had not lived at home with my parents in a very long time. At forty-six years old, I felt I was too old to live back at home, and I believed every grown man needed to have a place he could call his own.

After some prayer and giving it some thought, however, I decided to go home. After five long years of incarceration, it felt quite surreal finally being able to walk outside those prison walls. My mom and dad were awaiting my release, and met me at the front gate, receiving me with open arms. My brother, Dion, loaded up the car's back seat full of new clothes, hats and shoes that I quickly changed into in the car. The last thing I wanted to do was look like I had just gotten out of the joint. And, through it all, I couldn't hide my demeanor or emotions.

During some of the most intense years of my addiction, I had lost loved ones that were dear to my heart. Daddy, Granny, Aunt Jeri, Uncle Stacy, and my cousin Monie had all transitioned on to the next level of their spiritual journeys. Sadly, because I had been caught in the clutches of my addiction, I was unable to say my final goodbyes or pay my respects to them.

Because only God can search the heart of man, He knew that regret, guilt, and shame had been cast upon me from the enemy. I knew that as angels watched over me from above, during my seemingly insurmountable troubles, they asked the Father for His protection by continuing to hide me under the shadow of His wing.

Coming back home and not having had my mom and dad in my daily life was very uncomfortable to deal with, but I could feel each one of them pulling for and encouraging me to try my hardest to get myself back together. I had been given a reprieve, and I was optimistic about my chances of getting it right this time.

The first phone call I made was to my daughter, Ceara, who was then thirty-one years old. No sooner than she answered the phone and her sweet voice fell softly upon my ears, all I could do was weep tears of joy.

Ceara, Ashlee and three of my grandchildren, who I laid eyes on for the first time, met me at home. Oh, my God! What love and exuberant affection my grandchildren and I had immediately for one another. What I felt at that moment was a feeling I had never experienced or even knew existed. There was no drug or pill that could ever duplicate or replicate the feeling that came from being with the people who loved me regardless of my faults.

I found a new way of making up for my absence in most of my kids' lives, by being a better grandfather than I was as a father.

Ramiyah, who we lovingly call "Cupcake," has the brightest eyes and most vibrant personality of my grandchildren. I'm sure my daughter, Ashlee, coached them on what to address me as, but I quickly became "PawPaw." It reminded me of my late grandfather, Lewis C. Hanserd, who was "the original" "PawPaw." Suddenly, I had conquered a new milestone in my troubled life; the blessing of becoming a grandparent.

It took me some time to get adjusted to civilian life. I got set up with some social services and participated in group sessions at a mental health facility that would prove extremely useful in my re-entry into society.

After a couple of months, my brother, Nick, got me a plug in a prominent barber shop in the community. When the owner interviewed me and told me that he had conducted a background check on me, he asked, 'Why should I give you a chance and jeopardize my business on someone with a past like yours?'

He had a valid point, because all I had was a certification in cosmetology and a life full of broken promises. So, there was no disputing the fact that I could become a threat to his livelihood and a possible liability to his growth and development.

I explained that I had turned a corner on my past life and just needed one chance to prove my integrity, character and worth. To this day, I believe that God had the final say on the owner's decision, because the following morning, he gave me a shot.

When I showed up, a station had been set up for me with all the clippers, combs, sanitation and hair products, smocks, and capes I would need to get the job done; all provided by the owner to me, at no cost. Look at how God was working in my life. Not only had He blessed me with an opportunity, but He also provided everything I needed to be successful at my craft.

During my first day at the shop, I made a little over two hundred dollars; all for doing something I quite honestly enjoyed. At the end of the day, when I returned home, I called the owner to tell him how my day had gone. Shortly after, he stopped by the house and picked up the day's rent for my booth, and we established a weekly fee. I, again, thanked him for giving me a shot and, once again, promised not to disappoint him for the chance he was taking on me.

Over time, I developed a regular clientele, and the money was good. I remember, there was once a time, when ten dollars would have given me the desire to run and get high. Now, money was no longer a trigger for my drug use, and I was beginning to see that it was possible to live a life without drugs, alcohol, or cigarettes. My days consisted of working, going to church, and staying focused on making sound and wise decisions to keep me on the right path going forward.

As my life continued to evolve, I wasn't even involved in a sexual relationship with anyone. I prayed that, in God's time, He would bring a woman into my life that deserved a good brother like me. And then, He did just that.

One day, while riding around with my cousin, Nicky, somehow, we ended up, unannounced, at Kemra's condo. When she opened the door, we cordially embraced and then she took me to see her mother, Erma, who I have always loved. It was also the first time I met her grown son, Donovan. After visiting for a short time, I got Kemra's phone number, and then Nicky and I left.

Though Kem had told me that she wasn't a big talker on the phone, we ended up talking every day for hours sometimes. Within days, I invited her to come over, so I cook dinner for her. After spending all day making my famous, original lasagna recipe, about an hour before dinner, Kem called and disappointingly told me that an out-of-town family member required her attention, and she wouldn't be able to make it. She did, however, offer instead to take me to the movies and out to eat the following weekend.

Mom was about to go to Phoenix that weekend but, before she left, she lovingly told me not to be upset if things didn't work out again. Preparing for my evening with Kemra, I got as fly as I could and, when she arrived, I opened the door to see the most beautiful and sophisticated black woman I had ever laid eyes on.

Communication between Kemra and I had never been a problem, as we had been friends all our lives. As we walked into the movie theater, surrounded by bright lights and large mirrors, Kem saw the reflection of a couple in the mirror and said out loud, 'That's a good-looking couple.' To my amusing agreement, the image in the mirror was the two of us.

We sat down to watch 'Barbershop 2,' and shared a box of popcorn and dessert. At the end of our first date, because I was extremely nervous, it concluded with a quite awkward kiss; a kiss, however, that would end up being the first of many to come.

Kemra and I saw quite a bit of one another, as we slowly crossed the point of no return from friendship to falling in love. Kem told me that it had been some time since she had been in a relationship, and that she wanted to wait until she was married before she had sex again.

Though I was taken aback, somewhat, it quickly dawned on me that I had never been in a relationship that required any sort of sacrifice or commitment. As I thought of Kemra and just how much love I was beginning to feel for her, I told myself, "I believe she's worth it."

Though Kemra's request was generally viewed as old-fashioned, I really began to feel more respect for myself in accepting our abstinence; even though it was difficult trying to find that thin line between showing her that I was physically attracted to her while, at the same time, not crossing the "gun line."

After four months, we got married. It wasn't the wedding we had hoped for, but it was sweet and special, because our parents were there for us, along with the Pastor, his wife, and his secretary. And as we repeated our vows, I thought of God, my heavenly Father, who had, once again, blessed me with one of the desires of my heart. That's when tears of joy flooded my soul; my dream of marrying Kemra became a reality.

It felt so wonderful having such a loving, caring, strong and beautiful black woman to call my own. It had been over twenty years since I had been in a relationship with a sister, and things were different now.

Some of the "B.S." I usually got away with, Kem quickly rebuffed. She let me know, without mincing words, she wanted more out of me, and she absolutely wasn't about to settle for anything less. As a result, I found myself becoming a better man domestically, morally, and ethically.

Now I will admit that these new changes were foreign characteristics to me, but I wanted to be a family man and the head of the house. I knew I could trust in my wife, because she had my back, and her best intentions for me were the foundation for everything on which we were trying to build together.

Was everything in my life finally perfect? No, but most of it was good and I was, for the moment, experiencing life again, instead of merely existing in it.

Chapter 10

Addicted to the Game

B ecause I had been living my prior life so precariously, there were now real-life issues that I had not had to face before. I realized being married was not as easy as I thought or made myself believe it would be.

Instead of taking the adult approach to resolve some of the ordinary issues couples have, I played the victim and decided, most of the time, to avoid them all together. Kemra tried to help me see the other side of each conflict, but I'm sure, out of frustration, she usually gave up and most of our problems were left unresolved, and they began to compound, one on top of the other.

I won't allow myself to bear all the blame for our problems, however, nor will I throw Kem under the bus, because 'it takes two to tango.' Kemra's problems, which included jealousy, insecurity, trust issues that were injuriously inflicted and caused from previously relationships and being used to controlling and manipulating her significant others, were just a few issues of hers that countered all of mine.

During a disagreement, there's rarely a conclusion that determines "who's right" or "who's wrong." There are, however, common denominators that are needed in order to come to a compromise. One is to, at least, admit to yourself when you know you are wrong. Another is to understand the opposite party's point of view and perspective, or just agree to disagree. Mature, open-minded adults usually take one these approaches and move on.

The majority of my own ignorance stems from being locked up. There have been no programs, groups or classes made available to educate detained individuals on real life issues.

The university that I had the privilege of graduating from didn't offer any education relating to any of that. Their "school of hard knocks" philosophy was "get yours by any means necessary, no matter the cost.

About six months into my marriage, I drank one beer on a special occasion. Immediately feeling its effects, I quickly embraced the memory of what it felt like being intoxicated. A couple of beers here, a couple of beers there, along with one bad disagreement, led me back to my former mistress, cocaine, who had been waiting on me all along. Almost cat-like in her presence, she was patient, quiet and ready to pounce. In the back of my mind and in the bottom of my heart, there was no denying where I was headed. I was doomed from day one.

Even though I did my best to fight it off and tried to stand my ground, there was a crack in the foundation of where I stood. The water had slowly begun to creep in and soon, the levee would break, and the flood of addiction would consume me.

I quickly lost my job at the barbershop, due to a dispute with the owner over what I should and could not charge for my services. So, I started cooking again and received a competitive wage. Yet, when the hours weren't adding up, I began a general labor job in a peanut factory on the outskirts of town.

I worked hard and started playing even harder. Before too long, I left home and got an apartment back on the land. And then, of course, on the side, I began selling drugs, pimpin' and stealing to feed the overgrown gorilla riding my back, once again. It was as though I had never left. I was back at "rock bottom" and, once again, addicted to the game.

I had my parole officer fooled or, truth be told, he most likely didn't care. I was avoiding my wife and our marriage which, to me, felt like it was all over. And, as always, the streets once again embraced me, and I reconnected with gang members, dope boys and hookers to find my way back to where I comfortably seemed to fit in.

Somehow, I also developed quite an extensive line of credit with my suppliers. Because they knew that I was always getting money, it was to their advantage to keep their hooks in me and not have any reason to turn me loose.

The devil had me just where he wanted me again; in a position to kill me. The streets, though, had drastically changed; now, there was a heroin epidemic in progress. Men and women, young and old, were suddenly overdosing daily on heroin, fentanyl, elephant tranquilizers and other deadly chemicals and poisons.

I had invited a young brother to come by the apartment, because we had a similar interest in the same girl. She had chosen to be with me, and he and I needed to work it out as men before it turned into something else. To our credit, the brother and I were able to hash out our differences.

During the time we spent talking, I learned that this young brother had just been released from jail and was fresh back out on the streets. What I didn't know was that he had snorted a line of some toxic-laced heroin, while he was in my home. Thinking he had simply nodded off, after some time when he didn't wake up, it dawned on me that the brother had overdosed and died, in my living room, right in front of me.

In a week's time, he would be the first of three individuals to overdose at a location, where I happened to be. I suddenly began to fear that the police would start looking at me, suspecting that I was selling bad heroin. Because I didn't use it and was always around everyone who did, it made me a prime candidate to be supplying the land with this deadly poison, they so extremely craved and desired.

I suppose I could have talked our problems out with my wife and possibly returned home, but something inside of me would not allow my spirit to be forgiving or willing to man up. Getting help and asking for forgiveness, on my own behalf, never entered the equation.

At this point, I had not had any police contact, but I knew they were watching me because my landlord had come by the apartment with photos of surveillance footage the police had given him. They were watching my apartment and monitoring the drug traffic as prostitutes and gang-related patrons scurried back and forth through my doors.

Though it didn't come as a surprise, the landlord asked me to leave. Since I didn't have a lease, I found myself homeless again. What made this all so ironic was that I had a three-bedroom home, with my name on the lease and a beautiful wife to whom I could have retuned. But, as crazy as it might sound, I was alright with my predicament because I had been in this same jam a thousand times before. I knew the streets and, no doubt, had the game to make it.

I was in and out of most of the 'big box stores" in the far-east business district of town. I was also experimenting with selling pills, as they were the new craze among the youth. I didn't have a desire to sell heroin because it was the main culprit for taking so many lives at the time; besides, I didn't want to catch a drug-induced homicide.

In another attempt to turn my life around, I tried a thirty-day treatment program again and even went back home for a while. But, let's face it, I just could not and would not get myself back together. Following the Fourth of July weekend, I woke up in a psychiatric hospital in Des Plaines, Illinois. My body had all but shut down from exhaustion and a near overdose on cocaine and alcohol.

When I was finally discharged, Kemra came and picked me up. No sooner than we got into the truck, we began arguing, and did so all the way back to Rockford. As soon as we were back on the land, I never made it home because I got out of the truck and went my own way. All the trust Kem had in me was gone, and our marriage was in a terrible space, because my addiction made us both miserable.

A couple of weeks later, during a drunken, drug-binged night, I committed another series of armed robberies to fund this crazy rollercoaster of a ride I was on. As fate would have it, I was apprehended the next night and placed in custody at the Winnebago County Jail.

The next morning, following my arrest, I was so sick from withdrawal that I couldn't even appear at my court arraignment. But the day after that, when I felt well enough to face my charges, who did I lay eyes on? Kemra, of course. She was the first to be at my side to see about me and to show her support. The strange part about all of this was, I had not made one phone call to Kemra or anyone else to let them know what had transpired before my court appearance.

> When my arraignment ended, from the
> back of the courtroom, Kemra gave me a
> hand signal to call her. When I returned
> to my cell block and checked the kiosk,
> Kemra had placed three hundred dollars
> on my books. I couldn't believe it. After
> all I had put her through, she still found it
> in her heart to have love, compassion, and
> concern for me.

The county jail was hard time, and I was extremely worried about the sentence the state would seek to give me, this time around. The numbers they were offering were way too high, and this put an even greater strain on our marriage. So, after about ten months, Kem decided to file for divorce, and, eventually, it was granted. She filed under "irreconcilable differences" and the inability for it to be contested.

I just wish we could have had the chance to try some sincere marriage counseling and, maybe, we could have found some other alternatives to save our marriage, before throwing in the towel. We married "for better or for worse," but the worse had gotten the better of us. Yet, no matter what our outcome entailed, Kem promised to be with me every step of the way.

I couldn't get my charges lowered or be made eligible for probation or some kind of special court at all. The State of Illinois was truly tired of seeing me come and go, so I was not surprised at all that it had come down to this.

I was sentenced to eighteen years and sent to a behavioral modification facility, the first of its kind in Illinois. Working hard to become mentally stable again, I worried and wondered if I could bounce back from this devastating chain of events. I hoped and prayed that I could, but only God knew, for sure if I would.

Chapter 11

Cloudy Vision

As I began my mental health treatment, I decided to bear my feelings and begin sharing some of the issues that were plaguing me. Fortunately, I found myself in the presence of some very positive brothers, who became very influential in my recovery. We wrote poetry, sang songs, listened to music, and participated in a lot of group therapy.

I soon acquired the assignment as the resident barber and found favor among the staff, administration, and correctional officers. Being the sole barber in the facility led to a very good hustle, but my workload was phenomenal. At times, I was cutting twenty-five or more residents' hair a day and, before I knew it, the work became exhausting. So, I made a power move to get another brother hired alongside of me. I threatened that if my request, to lighten my workload, didn't meet their approval, I would walk off the job. I found this as an opportunity to open the door for another brother who was qualified to do the job but wasn't allowed to have the chance to do the work because he didn't have any credentials.

I have always been partial to our people, even though I don't hold everything against the white man that has to do with our present struggles. Once I began to admit that my personal choices were the ultimate reason for my own plight, that's when the wheels began to turn on how to elevate myself above them.

I submerged myself into the facility's mental health program and became a mentor to those who came in behind me, as well as those who continued to struggle with their own personal and mental health issues. I took a vocational course and even got involved in some leisure time activities. I also made a commitment to lose twenty-five pounds off my body weight. Financially, I was struggling, but the Lord continued to make a way for me, anyway.

Peace had finally come me, as I started to experience being "free on the inside." This metaphor displays the mind, soul, and spirit, allowing one to achieve liberty from the bondage of addiction, mental illness, low esteem, depression, and all other sorts of wiles devised by the enemy, to keep you in a state of disillusionment. It also prevents your inability to receive what God has created for you in order to escape the battlefield that is erupting in your mind.

I realize that, even if you're living a regular life, you don't have to be incarcerated to be locked up and taken as a prisoner in chains. Deliverance can only come from God above. Receiving a breakthrough is often like the children of Israel not being able to step one foot into the Promised Land, even when it was right in front of them.

Fear is one of the devil's greatest weapons. It is what I believe to be the most dangerous and responsible emotional tactic created for denying brothers and sisters the spiritual freedom they so desire and deserve.

I was beginning to receive pieces of my life back, but I wanted it more abundantly. I refused to settle with just being all right. I always knew that God had a plan over my life that included greatness, so ninety-nine and a half percent just wouldn't do!

I went on to become the first inmate to complete the pilot program for behavioral therapy. The doctors in charge of the program, my personal psychiatrist and the Prison

Warden voted unanimously that I had successfully met all the requirements outlined. They also believed that I would be a fantastic candidate to prove that the program was indeed useful and beneficial. I was honored by their recommendation because it allowed me to be even more confident in my ability to be all I could be, and all that God wanted me to be.

In Joel 2:25 (KJV), the Word of God says, 'So I will restore to you the years that the swarming locust has eaten.' My condition had been like a malignant cancer eating away at my life. It had slowly destroyed many aspects of it, but it had not been able to totally take away the hope that, one day, I would rise from the ashes. That would be the day when the true beauty inside of me would shine a vibrant reflection of God's goodness and his still ever-present healing power.

When I eventually transferred to a general population prison, about an hour and a half away, I wasn't really phased by the transition, because my history with the Department of Corrections was extensive.

I was now around a larger group of individuals, all different, with various agendas, personalities, aggression levels and demons. Instead of solely being focused on therapy and self-improvement I, now, had to get on point defensively, as the personal safety I had recently taken for granted, had suddenly been taken away.

Before I left the treatment facility, my biological father, William, passed away. Complications from a stroke had left him in a nursing home for some years, until he ultimately ended up dying alone. Resentment from my brother Michael, and my sister Treece, left him without one of his children to say goodbye to him. I, being in prison and unable to go, was hurt, and I took it harder than most could have ever expected or imagined.

You see, over the years, William and I had developed a relationship after he quit using drugs. He tried hard to share his wisdom and instruction to help me find God, with the hope that it would steer me away from trouble that always seemed to plague my every step.

Over the years, I was able to see just how much I was like William. Throughout my addiction, I was also able to recognize how my relationship with my children reflected the relationship William had with Michael, Treece and me. So, that old saying, 'the fruit doesn't fall far from the tree' is a simple and, sometimes, uncomfortable truth that follows many of us our entire lives. As a result, we get to a point where we must be willing to look in a mirror at ourselves and truthfully admit to the image we see, on how we became that person, and what we must do to become a catalyst for change.

Now that I was in my new prison, I quickly noticed that drugs, alcohol, homosexuality, and indifferences about God were some of the biggest ongoing issues that troubled the facility.

Because I was a Christian, I became a part of the minority and was looked down upon among most black inmates. The thought was and is that "the art of not fighting back" was instilled in us by our oppressors and, if you continued adhering to that, you could count on being continually oppressed through authoritarian treatment.

After a while, I was introduced to "the knowledge of self." I was shown, fact after fact, on how "my God" was a mystery God, who truly did not exist. I won't lie, but most of the information I read and received was very difficult to dispute or to even disagree with. As the material began to sour and dampen my spirit, I became angry and bitter. It was as though my soul had been infiltrated, and the space I was in was no longer peaceful nor fruitful.

I took two steps backwards from all the progress I had made, just a few months before, in treatment. Mentally, I was a mess, and I started to blame everyone for my present state and condition. As my life began unraveling and my support system was ready to desert me because of my constant complaining and negativity, my peers were telling me that I was the author of my own destiny, and things would only get better for me if I, alone, made them that way.

Prayer, devotion and requested assistance from God had been eliminated from my life, and a spiritual desert became my habitat. Pain, anger, and loneliness became my closest friends, while I wandered around from day to day, allowing my time to do me, instead of me doing my time. The reality was, the light at the end of the tunnel had been snuffed out, and I roamed around in seemingly total darkness within my own spirit.

The word of God says, 'The joy of the Lord is your strength.' Once again, my joy had been stolen by the enemy. I had removed my spiritual armor, and I was in the middle of defeat in the face of my adversary.

Then, one morning during a moment of despair, I called my mom and told her that I was ready to give up on God. I felt my life had been a wreck for too long. I couldn't understand why all my troubles had to happen to me. Why and what did I do to deserve everything the devil dragged me through most of my life?

Mom told me, 'Don't give up on God, yet!' She also suggested that I call my Aunt Pat to talk with her. I had about a dollar on my phone credit, and I used it to call her. As usual, she was a good listener, and then she gave it to me without regards for my feelings or misguidance that were causing my disbelief and lack of faith.

Aunt Pat suggested that I read something positive about God and try to pray. I had no praying life, at this time, and my Bible was buried at the bottom of a storage box. Suddenly, I remembered that, during one of my previous incarcerations, Aunt Pat had sent me a daily devotional that I found a copy of, among my other buried belongings, which were stored in a dayroom closet.

After shedding some tears as I listened to Aunt Pat's encouragement and positive reinforcement, I hung up the phone, went to the closet, and dug out the book, "Streams in the Desert." As I read the passage of the day, the spirit of the Living God began to speak to me. The passage was exactly what I needed to hear. It was evident the message had been inspired through the author and published just for me to read, at the very moment and time in my life, when I needed it most.

I felt as if I had been allowed to be close enough to Jesus to touch the hem of his garment. Immediately, a light had been lit in my soul and spirit, which gave me the ability to turn around and head in the opposite direction. God did not hesitate in lifting me back upon higher ground. I serve a "right now God," who, without warning, can show up and strike any of us like a bolt of lightning before we know what has hit us.

The next morning, feeling full of God's light, I found myself encouraging another brother, who also was in despair. I made the decision to blot out all the negativity, complaining and ungratefulness that had been so much a part of my life. The adage, 'You reap what you sow,' held true. The more positivity I put out into the universe, the more positive things started flowing back into my life.

I saw an increase in every area of my life and, as a result, I started to feel like Steve again. My trust in God returned, and hope had been restored in my life.

"If any man be in Christ, he is a new creature. Old things are passed away, behold all things are made new." (2 Corinthians 5:17)

Chapter 12

Bridge Builder

There was a man who lived in a troubled land. One day, he decided to take a journey to a peaceful destination, where his troubles would no longer plague him. Finding the road that would take him there, as he walked along, he came upon a gigantic hole that prevented him from going any further.

Sitting down, at the foot of a mountain, by the side of the road, he carefully pondered his options. Returning from whence he came was not one of them, so he looked up at the mountain and knew what he had to do. He began clawing and struggling in his quest to climb and cross over the mountain and, after quite some time, he successfully made it to the other side. As he looked around, seeing the joy and freedom from his prior struggles that awaited him, he realized how much better life would be for him now.

Even though he had reached the other side, instead of basking in the moment and jumping right into his new life, he decided to climb back down the mountain and return to the road, where he would build a bridge across the gigantic hole.

Now, other people at his new destination, who had seen him and were there to greet him, asked, 'Where are you going, and why would you go back after all you went through to get here?'

He told them that there were many others trapped in the place from which he had come, so he was going to build a bridge that would help them get there, as well.

Most people will say that you should disassociate yourself with all ties that you were entangled with, during your past, in order to protect and defend yourself against the same triggers and pitfalls that can easily threaten your future.

As far as I am concerned, until you are strong enough to evade any temptation that may arise from memory or nostalgia, I agree. The reason God gives you freedom and grants you liberty from an affliction, is not to go on your way and act as if nothing ever happened to you. He does it so that you will be fully equipped to aid and assist others through their similar trials, whether it be by hands-on assistance or allowing your testimony to reach them and help them through their troubled time.

My prayers started to include asking God to restore and rebuild the relationships between my children, grandchildren, and family members. I also prayed that God would restore my marriage to Kemra if He saw fit for me to be blessed in a reunion with her.

After some time, I was able to place two of my daughters, Ceara and Ashlee, on my phone list. Being able to speak to them and reconnect with my grandchildren was truly a blessing. Once again, the Lord was proving to be a bridge builder in my life. The relationships between me and my children had begun to take on new life and meaning.

I realized, now that they were grown, they were making decisions on how to live their own lives, raise their own children and provide for their own families.

As I have gotten older, I identify more with the fact that my parents continue to play a far more vital role in my life. This is a realization that comes from maturity and wisdom, along with the act of admitting that I have, yet, to acquire all that I need to understand and make all the right choices in my own life.

The fact that I was physically able to let my kids know that I, indeed, loved them and always had, was enough for me, at that time. One of my main problems has always been that I do not allow God to do His job without assistance or interference from me.

I have a bad habit of getting in the way, trying to control and manipulate things that He is in the process of personally taking care of. This is a matter of trust and becoming impatient in allowing God to do exactly what He promised and taking Him at his word.

I was eventually moved to a housing unit reserved for older men, where things were quite different. Most of the men housed there had been locked up for the better part of twenty years or more. These inmates, around me, had either been sentenced to life or probably weren't going to be young when they finally reached the end of their sentences. But there was no way you would ever know that based on their demeanors or their attitudes.

In my new housing unit, I found myself back in a more respectful and positive atmosphere. Most of the men were either Christians, Muslims, or veterans of the U.S. Military.

By my being a lot younger than most and having had the chance to see the other side of a prison wall in recent years, I was a welcomed sight to them. In fact, a few individuals had even heard about me because of my gang affiliation and reputation, back in the day, when I was known as "Shorty," on the streets.

I didn't exactly develop a lot of personal relationships, but what I did do, I learned a lot by osmosis of what I had been doing wrong in my failed attempts to leave the street life and to quit going back and forth to prison.

God had given me chance after chance, to let go of all the wrong-doings I was entangled in, so that I could live a meaningful life that would reflect better on me and those I loved and cared about.

Oh, how I realized that I had so brutally taken advantage, time after time, of the opportunity to change and stay out of prison. I know, without a doubt, every man in my housing unit would have gladly traded in their lives to have the chance to walk through those prison gates.

Sadly, I witnessed a few individuals die from illness and old age. It showed me that only because of God's grace, I had been allowed to continue breathing the breath of life. It also gave me hope that all I was now learning and seeing would be all I needed to complete a lesson that I had so painfully and purposely ignored, at the times I needed it most. With an eerie feeling looming over me, I knew that, if I didn't get it right this time, this would be the final act for me.

After a period, I, methodically, began to receive the refreshing fruits of the spirit once more. As the seven attributes (love, peace, joy, gentleness, longsuffering, goodness, and faith) of God's Spirit were introduced to my soul, I found such a blessing in being awakened every morning, so that I could bear witness to my God's faithfulness. I also requested God to send someone along my path that day that I could encourage, bring a little hope to, or tell of His gospel.

I was a man who had, once, been responsible for hurting and destroying the lives of others. Now, I was being enlisted by the Master to do his work and spread the message by example, through word and deed. That gave me so many reasons to feel better about myself.

After all I had done and been through in the past, I felt like being in Christian service gave me the balance I sorely needed on the scale of my life. I became infinitely proud of the life I was aspiring to live. With the devil placed far beneath me, my life took on new meaning as I came to the realization that my victory was and always had been in Jesus.

My financial situation also had a new light shed upon it as I experienced blessing after blessing, from month to month. My trust in the Lord was easier to achieve, and I recognized that it was time to put my old life behind me and trust God to open a new direction for me.

After some thought and plenty of prayer, I decided to relocate from Illinois to Arizona, because I felt it would be a great place for a new start, after my incarceration.

Now remember what I earlier stated about fear. I prayed to God that, through my "fear of the unknown and total blind faith," He would open doors and create avenues for me. Once those opportunities were made available to me, my greatest obstacles would be any fear or blind faith that I might allow to control or hinder me from being my best self. After all, God had not brought me this far to return me to the muck and mire that had me stuck in an endless rut, in which I repeatedly found myself. I know, without a doubt, that God is a "way maker," and I felt blessed, more than I can say, to know that through His grace, He was giving me the gift of "making a new way" for myself. It was his way of proving to me that, no matter how my bad life had once been, His love for me never wavered.

But then on January 26, 2020, the shocking news came that NBA All-Star and former Los Angeles Laker, Kobe Bryant, along with his 13-year-old daughter, Gianna, and seven other passengers, had been killed in a horrific helicopter crash in Calabasas, California. The devastating news stunned the world. In some way, it also seemed to set into motion the beginning of a new decade and year that would historically become one of the worst I have ever personally witnessed and lived through.

When I initially learned about Kobe's death, I had received the news from a brother named Ford, who lived in my housing unit. I was so stunned that I had to leave the dayroom and retire to my own quarters. It seemed, no matter which channel I turned to, every television station was providing endless coverage that seemed to get worse, by the minute, as more information became available about the victims.

My spirit was heartbroken! For as long as I could remember, Kobe seemed to be a part of me. I had followed him, his life and incredible career from day one, when he arrive in Los Angeles to play for the Lakers. The thought of him and his daughter being taken away from us weighed heavily on me.

Trying to make some sense of a tragedy that, from all indications, should not have happened, my thoughts immediately went directly to my own daughters, Ceara, Ashlee and Lasha. Their importance in my life was magnified exponentially, and it was at that very moment the harsh reality that my relationships with my children had been taken for granted and squandered, came front and center for me.

Had it not been for God's "grace" and "mercy" that have always been showered down upon us, it could just as easily have been me and my children going through the same tragedy.

As I mourned the deaths and prayed for the Bryant Family, I initiated a more fervent prayer regarding the relationships between me and my children. Kobe's death had been the most tragic loss of any African American icon of my generation. Not even the death of rapper Tupac (2Pac) Shakur had such an emotional impact and painful toll on our world as Kobe's did.

Then, wouldn't you know, just as I was recovering from the news about Kobe, I ended up developing a hernia that caused me some health issues. I was transferred from the senior housing unit to one, where I could be placed in a lower bunk, to help me from making my ailment any worse.

After adjusting and continuing with the daily routine of my incarceration, 2020 reared its ugly head again with the most unbelievable catastrophe that, without a doubt, changed the entire world forever. A little-known virus had caused an outbreak of respiratory illness cases in Wuhan City, Hubei Province, China that, in a short amount of time, would ultimately infect one country after another, with no respect nor limitations to one's nationality or race.

This deadly virus known as Covid-19 or Coronavirus swept through the world like a thief in the night, shutting down the entire planet. Life, as the world knew it, was stopped in its tracks, and this invisible enemy quickly snowballed into a force of nature unconceivable to mankind.

Considered far more contagious and deadlier than the Bubonic Plague of 1346 and the 1918 Influenza pandemic, Covid-19 has touched every region of the world, forcing all countries into immediate quarantine and imminent lockdowns.

Sports arenas were emptied, along with schools, churches, workplaces, businesses and, who would have ever thought we would live to see "no signs of human life on any street" in the entire world?

The stark images of unbelievable suffering and carnage that had, until now, been seen only in fictional, epic Hollywood productions would, sadly, end up becoming a tragic universal reality without the usual happy Hollywood ending.

At the prison, we went on lockdown and were only allowed out of our cells for an hour a day, until further notice.

What might have been the saddest footnote to this entire pandemic is that the "court jester" and "carnival barker,"

Donald Trump, who America voted to be President of our United States, so deliberately and falsely promised that his administration had the virus under control, and all would be fine, soon.

To date, nearly 750,000 Americans have died from Covid-19. And, while the former Oval Office Idiot's indifference and selfish, political desire to be re-elected held more precedence and importance over savings lives, it's no wonder that his totally false and insensitive statement, 'There is nothing to worry about' has proven to all of us that 'there will always be plenty to worry about as long as the Coronavirus and its variants continue ravaging America and the rest of the world.

Chapter 13

I Can't Breathe

May 25, 2020 - will forever be emblazoned as another despicable chapter in both Black and American history books. It is the day George Floyd, an unarmed black man in Minneapolis, Minnesota, was murdered after being accused of trying to spend a counterfeit twenty-dollar bill for a pack of cigarettes at a local corner store.

Floyd, who was handcuffed and lying face-down on the street, beside a police car, offered no signs of resistance, as Minneapolis Police Officer, Derek Chauvin, subdued him with a knee on his neck for 9 minutes and 29 seconds. Throughout his ordeal, according to publicly released transcripts, Floyd pleadingly told Chauvin more than twenty times, 'I can't breathe.' Yet, as Chauvin nonchalantly placed his hands in his pockets, then shifted his weight and pressed his knee further down into Floyd's neck, George urgently cried out to his mother, who had died two years earlier.

With his breath becoming shallower by the second and foam oozing from his mouth, Floyd instinctively needed to tell his mother he loved her, because he was gradually fading into a state of unconsciousness that would lead to his death.

Chauvin, indifferent to Floyd's pleas and to those of frantic witnesses on the scene, intentionally continued applying his lethal and illegal chokehold, even as cell phone cameras and nearby surveillance cameras captured the injustice from beginning to end.

It is unconscionable that as the murder of George Floyd happened at that busy intersection in a black community, gathering witnesses (men, women, and children) were being held off at gunpoint and verbally threatened by accompanying officers, as they pleaded with Chauvin to allow Floyd to be able to stand and regain his breath.

As Chauvin arrogantly eyed the frantic crowd, and George laid lifeless on the pavement, little did Chauvin know that, within hours, the entire world would see nonstop, shocking accounts of Floyd's death. And, in the days that followed, the world would begin to see case after case of how America has intently allowed its persistent and systemic racism to adversely affect and destroy black and other people of color from one generation to another.

The murder of George Floyd sparked waves of protests throughout the world. And while most protests were organized and peaceful, dissention and resentment among smaller and less peaceful troublemakers sparked powder keg incidents that erupted into violence and riots in nearly every city throughout the country. These "so-called" United States of America had become a "Divided States of America," with no back-up plan or intention to become reunited.

What made America's eruption over Floyd's death so volatile was the fact that the black community had long been "sick and tired" of continually watching their brothers and sisters die unjustly at the hands of police, who never were held accountable.

During a deadly pandemic that was beginning to firmly grip a country already panicked and edge, it seemed impossible that, at the same time, we could also be on the verge of what had the potential of becoming one of the deadliest riots this country has ever faced.

All I could do was watch as the riots unfolded on the television, day after day. I had no way of knowing how it would all end and, as tension escalated across our land, I became angrier and angrier. With tears falling from my eyes, I yelled with angst at white America and the great divide that plagued our great land.

Since the prison was already in quarantine, they were only allowing two guys at a time to be out of their cells for thirty minutes every forty-eight hours. If we had been under normal operating procedures, God only knows what might have occurred.

My daughter, Ashlee, was living in Minnesota with five of my grandchildren and the father of her kids. I couldn't help but worry about their well-being and safety, considering that she was located so close to the epicenter of all this madness. And the truth is, I wished I could have been out there to assist and represent my people, by any means necessary.

Even my mother, who is an old-fashioned, traditional Missionary Baptist woman, who sits on the Mother's Board at her church, told me that she 'was glad that this generation was bold enough stand up for us because generations, before them, would not.'

Enough was enough! If white America wouldn't begin to show that black lives mattered, then we wouldn't show any respect or regard for them either. How do you hurt or get even with someone who has, seemingly, everything? You find out what matters most to them and begin to destroy it! And that's exactly what was happening. Large parts of the United States were being destroyed, torn down and occupied not only by black folks and the Hispanic community, but there were many white folks who joined us in our fight against a racist system that seems to continually go out of its way to oppress and intentionally murder people of color.

Personally, although I grew up not really knowing what true racism was, I had noticed, for some time, that even Rockford had become a melting pot threatening to boil over. Much had changed from when our schools and neighborhoods were mixed, and my parents never taught us anything about the racism that existed, right outside our door.

My Mom and Dad tried to keep sensitive subjects and difficult conversations away from our home. They didn't teach me or my brothers about racism, drugs, sex, or the streets. Sure, we knew about those things but, ultimately, after being told they were "off limits" and "taboo," my curiosity usually led me straight down the path to learn as much as I could about it all.

Now, most of the Black and Hispanic brothers and sisters that I've met from larger metropolitan cities tend to be, somewhat, prejudice themselves. And, how else would I expect them to be? After all, their neighborhoods and schools were occupied solely by people of color, and all they grew up seeing and knowing was oppression by Jim Crow laws, white cops, and persistent division along racial lines. And, as much as many would like to believe that segregation is a problem known only to our Southern states, the reality is, it is just as prevalent in the Northern half of our country, from the east coast to west.

The seeds of hatred, prejudice and systemic racism know no bounds, and prisons are no exception as those same ills breed and flourish within the volatile grounds behind their walls. Sure, society's consensus tends to be, 'if people would quit committing crimes that send them to prison, then those issues wouldn't exist.' So, then, what does that say about that same society's reasons for its own never-ending social ills with one another?

One of the biggest burdens that has been put upon African Americans, throughout this country, are drugs and a proliferation of guns that have been purposely dumped within our communities for us to use against one another. And, when you factor in a lack of education, high unemployment rates, among countless other ills that are so familiar to many men and women in our inner cities, it's no wonder why they resort to the drastic measures they do in order to survive.

This country's most egregious and ongoing form of slavery is through its Department of Corrections. Housing nearly 2-1/2 million people in its prisons and jails throughout its fifty states, including every crook and cranny of rural America, gives this nation the dubious distinction as the world's leader in incarcerations.

In state prisons throughout America, African Americans are imprisoned at a rate of 5.1 times than white Americans. And in five states (Iowa, Minnesota, New Jersey, Vermont and Wisconsin, the imprisonment rate of African Americans to white Americans is more than 10 to 1. And, if we delve deeper into the disparity, the Department of Justice statistics show that in twelve states (Alabama, Delaware, Georgia, Illinois, Louisiana, Maryland, Michigan, Mississippi, New Jersey, North Carolina, South Carolina, and Virginia – "more than half" of their populations are black. Maryland, who tops the nation in the number of African Americans being held in their prisons, stands at 72%.

While many African American Americans have died at the hands of police, prior to the killing of George Floyd, the public's heated response to his intentional death by Derek Chauvin has not been enough to stop police, throughout this country, from taking further innocent lives. 2020, alone, will go down in history as an epidemic year of murders that would not have happened had the persons on the other end of those policemen's gun been white.

The murders of Breonna Taylor (Kentucky), Ahmaud Arbery (Georgia), Rayshard Brooks (Georgia), Daunte Wright (Minnesota) and the near-fatal shooting of Jacob Blake (Wisconsin), who was shot in the back at point blank range seven times, in front of his three young sons, are just a small accounting of the incidents that have continued in this country; in many instances, without any accountability.

Week by week, it appears there was a "breaking news" report of yet another incident; worse than the previous one. And as America's "first dictator" sat idly in the Oval Office, continually stoking the flames of racism, disrespect and disregard for African American lives, the dissention among the masses meant very little.

In a feeble attempt to bring a volatile situation under any semblance of control, government officials stood before the American people to create facades; to intentionally lie; and to perform publicity stunts for the sole purpose of their own personal political interests and agendas. The 'will of the people' had become irrelevant.

With an epidemic of police killings and a rampaging viral pandemic dominating the news, Mother Nature was not about to be upstaged; she had her own agenda. Seemingly, rising out of nowhere, fourteen deadly hurricanes caused more than $51 billion dollars in damages and claimed the lives of at least 417 people in 2020. Hurricanes had become so frequent that forecasting agencies were coming up with names like they were naming their newest family addition.

Now you probably won't believe this, but according to the National Interagency Fire Center, in 2020, there were 58,950 wildfires that ravaged nearly 10.1 million acres across America. We had our own "Hell on Earth," and now that we are well into 2021, the fires continue wreaking havoc, mainly upon our western states. The smoke from those fires have been and continue to be so dense, weather radars have shown how those fires have affected the air quality in the Midwest and across the country.

At one point, I emailed my Aunt Pat to discuss all the catastrophic events that were taking place at the same time around the world. I had never seen anything like it, and a quote from the 'Word of God' came to mind; 'the fervent prayers of the righteous availeth much.'

And that's just what I was doing; praying without ceasing. I entered a constant state of prayer, for only God could save us from all that we were going through. I know that prayer changes things. All throughout the history of the Bible, God was known to change His mind and some of

His decisions, due to someone going to him and pleading mercy on our behalf.

Being separated from an active lifestyle on the streets and in a position to live a righteous life, gave me a direct, uninterrupted line to Jesus Christ. I used him as my mediator to the Father, himself. I know that 'Faith without works is dead,' so I activated my faith in God and humbly gave him authority over all that was happening around me.

They say that 'patience is a virtue' and one thing I've developed, throughout my life of multiple incarcerations, is patience. You learn to wait for everything. You wait for court dates, you wait to eat, you wait to be let out of your cells, and you wait years for your release date; just to name a few.

One thing I have come to realize is that, on any given day we live, there are twenty-four hours in each day. If you learn to take it one day at a time, any short and long-term goals you have will come to pass.

When I was younger, I use to carelessly throw around the term, 'Lord, give me patience.' What I didn't know was that what I was actually praying for was for God to take me through something and allow me to learn how to endure it.

Nothing worth having ever comes easy. Now that I am an older, patience is a gift that I cherish as an old man. I know I can calmly await on God to do just as I trust him to do and just as He has always promised to do.

"Never have I seen the righteous forsaken, nor his seed begging for bread…"

Chapter 14

Fifty and Over

As Covid-19 continued to spread from one continent to another, there was not one nation invulnerable to the horrific devastation of its merciless clutch.

I began to worry about my own safety and went on high alert, even though we were on a 'Level One' lockdown. The thought of this ferocious, unseeable, microscopic entity's capability of ravaging through our prison community was the furthest thing from my mind.

What I could see, however, was being incarcerated at an Illinois prison proved what everyone of us already knew to be true; they didn't care one iota about our wellbeing.

The Center for Disease Control (CDC), the local health departments, and governors of every state quickly implemented protocols and mitigation strategies to protect the citizens of their communities.

The Illinois Department of Corrections, on the other hand, avoided every sanitizing measure, including issuing cleaning supplies for our living quarters, that the rest of the nation had begun adapting, to protect itself. The administration refused to test us, and what put our entire population in peril was the fact that guards and staff members were not being tested either; although they were allowed to continue to come to work, even after viral symptoms were shown to be present. Our meals were inadequately and improperly handled and served to us, and our health care system was all but totally shut down.

We were punished and treated very poorly and unfairly instead of being cared for and protected. Case after case of the virus began to mount one on top of the other and, before we knew it, the outbreak had become an out-of-control and uncontained firestorm,

We had no way of knowing who needed to be quarantined and who didn't, and we weren't even given the most general of information that could have informed us what was happening from day to day and how they intended to help us.

Day after day as we heard about the mounting loss of lives that were being lost to Covid-19, fear, uncertainty, and panic set in as the unknown future of us all placed an ominous veil over our lives. I did what I could to protect myself, my cellmate, and our living quarters. When the opportunity presented itself, I stole chemicals and used basic laundry detergent, hot water, and bath soap to clean my cell multiple times daily.

Meanwhile, every television channel's newscast was headlined by news of the pandemic, and it began to feel like the earth had stop spinning on its own axis.

As June 8, 2020, my fiftieth birthday approached, although the world around me was in chaos, it turned out to be a very special milestone for me. Somehow, through social media capabilities, namely Facebook, my mother put together a loving surprise on my behalf, when she invited people to wish me a 'Happy Birthday.'

Reflecting on my life, that day, I had been blessed with five children and eight grandchildren. Despite all the traps and snares placed before me, that could have ended my life, God saw fit to shine his Grace on me, so that I could live to see a half century.

The brothers I worked with daily, in the prison dietary department, laughed, joked, and teased me lovingly. A few of my younger brothers I was close to, in my housing unit, got together and cooked me an incredible meal of all-meat burritos, and they made a cake, which is considered a delicacy in prison, out of items they were able to obtain from the prison's commissary. Another young brother, named, "Dot" gave me a new pair of sneakers and had his wife send me a couple of dollars. Because I was working that day, I can't begin to explain how surprised I was, when I eventually returned to my cell.

That day, I received well over fifty birthday cards and letters in the mail. In fact, the prison guard, who worked my unit, told me that he had never seen one person's mail take up almost the entire mail bag at one time. I couldn't believe it! Mail came from as far as California, North Carolina, Minnesota, and Louisiana. I heard from friends, family, and strangers, I didn't even know, who reached out to me, in support through my mother.

One of my most memorable cards came from a young lady who said she went to high school with me, over thirty years ago. She wanted to thank me for having her back, when her brother, who was a friend of mine, had been killed. She said she had never forgotten it and how much it meant to her.

Her note brought tears to my eyes. After all I had done throughout the years and all I had been through, I had no idea so many people were still in my corner, willing to support me. Of all the birthdays I have lived to see, my fiftieth birthday, so ironically, turned out to be the best by far. Who knew, being locked up alone in a prison cell, that I would, on that day, be privileged to feel love from every corner of our great land?

Being able to believe in my heart that so many people still cared and were rooting for me gave me the much-needed push to confirm to myself that my life was, indeed, worth living.

That evening, the love of God came over me in my cell. Feeling as though every fiber of my being had been covered by His blood, I can honestly say, throughout my entire life, I had never experienced such a great outpouring of God's love.

As we all know, there is absolutely nothing, in this world, greater than a mother's love. Looking around my cell, cards were everywhere. I had placed them on the countertop desk, floor and on the wall. The evidence of my mother's love and that exhibited by her friends deeply moved me. With the feeling of my mother's arms wrapped around me, there was no question as to how very special I have always been and continue to be to her.

Chapter 15

Not Just Another
Lonely Christmas

We had seen and been through a horrific and riotous summer, and winter was coming! Just as the seasons change, so does everything in life. Nothing is ever truly constant but change.

Covid-19 continued its destructive path in my housing unit and throughout the prison, as well as everywhere else in the world. By that time, in the United States, alone, the staggering death toll had reached well over four hundred thousand, with no end in sight.

The Department of Corrections had finally been sued by an inmate for its failure to test the population for the virus. Subsequently, they were forced to contract an outside organization to test every inmate, staff members, medical professionals and officers, every three days, until the nemesis was phased out of our over-populated environment.

Right around this time, I had begun not feeling well. As the week progressed, I began experiencing a few additional symptoms that appeared to be Covid related, so I was tested for the virus. Not wanting to "wish bad on myself," I tried to remain optimistic about my pending test results.

Sadly, during this same time, my Aunt Lois was hospitalized and diagnosed with Covid Pneumonia. Frontline workers could not get her oxygen level up, and she went into a coma.

Immediately, after hearing of Aunt Lois's condition, I went deep into prayer, every morning, worshipping and beseeching the Father, on her behalf. I prayed the lyrics of "Breathe into Me, Oh Lord" by Fred Hammond. What we needed was the "Author and Finisher" of our faith to continue to breathe the breath of life into Aunt Lois's lungs, until they could get back to functioning properly on their own.

I called and checked on her status, daily, and the last word I received was that she was out of her coma, and that it looked like she was going to pull through and be okay.

Then, on Christmas Eve, because I wasn't feeling well, myself, I didn't call to inquire about Aunt Lois. Very early Christmas morning, I was informed that I had tested positive for Covid, and I was transferred to a quarantine building.

Later that morning, I was given the opportunity to call home to tell my mom about my condition and to wish her a 'Merry Christmas.' It was then that she dreadfully told me that Aunt Lois did not make it. She had passed on Christmas Eve.

I broke down. I couldn't believe that Aunt Lois didn't pull through. Losing her was another tragic loss to our family, as the realization settled in that we were not exempt from the out-stretched hands of the virus. It had fallen upon us and moved on to claim countless more lives.

Men were dying left and right around me, so the grim reality of the virus's relentlessness was not new to me. With my symptoms at a high, I had become severely ill and, suddenly, I was gripped with fear.

I went back to my cell and pulled out a family photo of Aunt Lois, Uncle Bobby, her son Duntai, daughter Tammy and grandson Martavion. I placed the photo on my desk and began to reminisce about Aunt Lois.

My mind drifted back to an early morning, in the early 1970's, when my cousin Duntai and I were about four or five years old. Aunt Lois happened to see us outside in our pajamas when we shouldn't have been. She came out of the house, searching everywhere. When she finally found us, she took us inside, and we both got whippings.

All my life, Aunt Lois never had one bad word to say about me or anyone else. She, along with my late Aunt Jeri, who passed years before, after a long battle with breast cancer, were always the sweetest women I had ever known.

As I was growing up and then becoming a teenager, Aunt Lois's home was an escape for me. I loved going to visit and, once I was there, I never wanted to leave. Being with Duntai, at Aunt Lois' house, was my definite favorite place in the world.

Now, her time on this earth was done, and God had abruptly decided to call her home. And as much as I wanted to be upset with God for taking her away from us, I just couldn't. Aunt Lois lived a good Christian life, and she left so many special memories for all of us to be able to call our own. She now had a much-deserved mansion in glory, and the privilege to hear the Master say, 'Servant, well done!'

Sick and all alone, it seemed that, once again, my world was collapsing around me; only this time, it wasn't by my own accord.

"The earth is the Lord's, and the fullness thereof; the world and they that dwell therein." (Psalm 24:1 KJV)

This was not just another lonely Christmas; it was the worst Christmas I had ever had. As I waded in the gloom around me, I forgot all about celebrating the birth of Christ. Death and sickness are human experiences that everyone deals with differently. I decided to remain grateful to God. I confessed in my heart and my spirit that He does not make any mistakes. I also realized that everything is by His design, and for His purpose, and it was not my place, as his child, to question him.

Chapter 16

New Management

T he next couple of days, I began to feel better. I was in the process of being transformed from the inside out. I took the critical situations of having Covid, being isolated for over a year, losing loved ones, and found positive resolutions to what was happening in my life and around me.

Now some of these decisions were difficult to make because most of them were lifestyle changes. Anyway, I'm not one to ever give up or doubt that I can overcome any obstacle. I weeded some negative people out of my cypher, who were simply dead weight, served no purpose to me, and certainly meant me no good.

I decided that a lot of the old things that I was being loyal to, for so long, didn't deserve my loyalty at all. They were merely unbeneficial obstacles holding me back. Over the course of my life, I had slowly become religious when it came to certain things. Most of my old concepts and theories also needed to be pruned. I had become stagnant at their hands and longed to be more productive, so that I could bear more fruit in my life.

I started studying psychology and relationship issues again, and I dove deep into the Word of God. The energy that changed my life was as instantaneous as microwaving a bowl of frozen food.

I shared a cell with a young brother from Chicago, who referred to himself as 'Knowledge.' There was a twenty-year age difference between us, and he believed in a culture known as the 'Nations of Gods and Earth.'

Although there was a vast difference between our beliefs, ages, and backgrounds, we quickly became quite compatible once we took the chance to get to know and understand one another. I found him to be very intelligent and poised for his age. He often joked about having an "old soul," some of which was true, but I allowed myself to remain open-minded as he talked and learned quite a bit from him.

A positive message related to friendship says, "Iron sharpeneth iron; so, a man sharpeneth the countenance of his friend" - (Proverbs 27:17 KJV). By the same token, I shared with him all the wisdom and experiences I had overcome throughout my life that would surely help him with his own.

Now, only one of two things happen when you're locked up in an eight-foot cell with someone for about twenty-four hours a day. You either wind up getting along or end up fighting. 'Knowledge' and I shared a part of life that will forever be an integral part of what changed me mentally, emotionally, and spiritually.

God won't come down and part the Red Sea, or turn water into wine, anymore, but what He continues to do, to this day, is provide miracles through other resources. Nothing happens by coincidence or because of a haphazard event.

My Aunt Margaret once told me, 'Stevie, God puts people in other people's lives, at certain times and for certain reasons, and when that purpose is complete, then you move on to the next chapter of your life.'

I'll forever be grateful to my God for giving me the blessing of being around this young brother. A healing took place in both of our lives.

So many obstacles are placed in our lives to cause a divide and to bridge a gap between people. If we can learn to look pass our differences, beliefs, backgrounds, gender, and race, what a better place our world would be to live in

We have heard it all before and even now; politicians polluting the atmosphere's empty space with petty lies and empty promises. At this point, sadly, we really have nothing else we can trust or hold on to in America.

Mr. Joseph Biden seems very sincere in his approach to cast hope into the homes across the country, about a better and brighter America; regardless of a person's political biases or persuasions.

I believe that God places rulers and people of authority in their positions. God heard the cry of America, when Joe Biden and our country's first black woman Vice President, Kamala Harris prevailed in the 2020 election. It just goes to prove, 'There is a balm in Gilead' to heal our land.

In early 2021, I went into surgery to have a procedure for a double hernia, and a second procedure for two non-cancerous lipomas. Up until then, I had never had any surgical procedure, other than to reset a broken arm, when I played football in middle school.

I was very apprehensive about how the procedures would go. I was treated at an outside hospital in Dixon, Illinois, and my medical team treated me superbly. I was handled with the same respect and care as any other citizen in the outside world, and not as a prisoner.

It all happened so fast. All I honestly remember was gently closing my eyes, and then waking up in recovery. Though the surgery seemed like it was over in just minutes, the surgery lasted five hours, and I was sent back to the correctional facility.

I begged and pleaded with the medical staff not to make me stay in the prison's infirmary, even though it meant I would have to make long walks to receive my medication and daily meals. I didn't care, after all, guys who were left alone in the prison hospital were not properly looked after and, oftentimes, they would die. I decided I would rather take my chances by being back in my own cell.

'Knowledge' and a handful of other guys, I was close to, looked after me and nursed me back to health. It was, during that time, that I decided to head down the road to the next chapter of my life and began composing this book.

I called my Mom and told her about my vision. We put our heads together, trying to come up with a title, but nothing natural or true came to mind so, I quickly went to the highest source and patiently waited on Him.

I knew the Lord would speak to my heart, to give me the appropriate title. Sure enough, not long after, I woke up one morning from a dream and clearly visualized the title, "Wounded."

"OK, Lord," I said, "that's it! Wounded." It was a profound and perfect metaphor for my life and those of black people, in general.

As I continued to meditate on the Word, what came next to mind was that nothing I have ever known in my life that was wounded and did not die, was healed. Some wounds are more severe than others, and some people and creatures take longer to heal than others. On the other hand, there are some who are never the same as before, and then there are some who never recover.

There are others who have been granted the privilege and the awesome opportunity to visit the Potter's House to be remade, reshaped and refashioned, to be better equipped to do His work and reach His people.

Truth be told, I should have been dead and gone a long time ago. Many, many times, the devil tried to kill me. There are many situations and circumstances that have not been told in this story, simply because of the need to protect certain individuals and myself from disrespect and incrimination.

God sent millions of ministering angels to protect and encompass themselves around me. *Love said not so.

This story of my life is one of change, fraught with difficulties, addiction, mental illness, multiple incarcerations, despair, thoughts of suicide, spirituality, and broken relationships; all of which were compounded by vanity, arrogance, ignorance, overcoming, healing, transformation, triumph, and victory, in the name of Jesus.

While, although, I know this story is my own personal journey, I realize that my story is, in no way, unique. There are many "lost souls," wandering around in the wilderness of life, wondering if they will ever make it to the Promised Land or be able to return to a life worth living.

My final statement to those "lost souls" is this: 'He bottles up every tear. He understands every fear. He knows the reasons why nights, we must sit and cry! For those reasons, its' why "we must put our trust in God."

Thank you, and may God bless everyone who took the time to read the story of my life. It was created just for you.

~Steven T. Hanserd ~

The End

*(Luke 15:21-22 & 24):

And (21) "the son said unto him, 'Father, I have sinned against heaven and against you. I am no longer worthy to be called your son.' (22) But the father said to his servants, 'Quick! Bring the best robe and put it on him. Put a ring on his finger and sandals on his feet. (24) For this son of mine was dead and is alive again; he was lost and is found.'

Writing my life story has been the most emotional experience I have ever encountered; reliving, having to confront and let go of my past. The creation of "Wounded" blessed me to be healed from a great many things. It has also put me in the position to draw strength from the Lord because I desperately needed to let go of my past, so I could move on with my life.

I want to give a special thanks to Sister Maxine Rhyne of Bethel Missionary Baptist Church, and a very special thanks to my editor, Joan Adrienne Sturgis, for allowing the Holy Spirit to touch their hearts and assist me, when I had no one else. I pray that as everything and everyone good comes into my life, from this day going forward, I will have the wisdom and the strength, every day, to embrace and learn all that God has ever wanted me to know.

Again, God bless you all!

* <u>Quotes from</u>: King James Bible and some anonymous.
* Some excerpts from songs by BeBe & CeCe Winans, and Fred Hammond

(Luke 15:21-22 & 24):

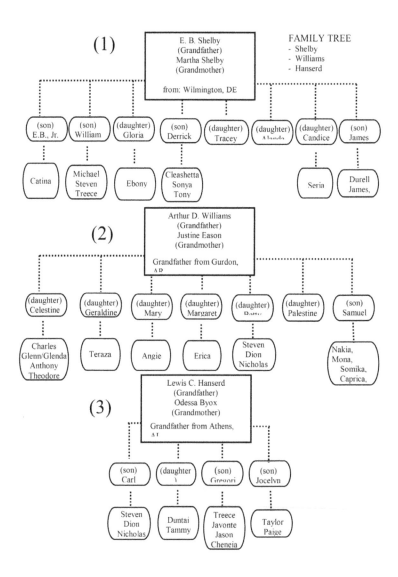

(1)

E. B. Shelby
(Grandfather)
Martha Shelby
(Grandmother)

from: Wilmington, DE

FAMILY TREE
- Shelby
- Williams
- Hanserd

| (son) E.B., Jr. | (son) William | (daughter) Gloria | (son) Derrick | (daughter) Tracey | (daughter) Alanda | (daughter) Candice | (son) James |

| Catina | Michael Steven Treece | Ebony | Cleashetta Sonya Tony | | | Seria | Durell James, |

(2)

Arthur D. Williams
(Grandfather)
Justine Eason
(Grandmother)

Grandfather from Gurdon,
AR

| (daughter) Celestine | (daughter) Geraldine | (daughter) Mary | (daughter) Margaret | (daughter) Betty | (daughter) Palestine | (son) Samuel |

| Charles Glenn/Glenda Anthony Theodore | Teraza | Angie | Erica | Steven Dion Nicholas | | Nakia, Mona, Somika, Caprica, |

(3)

Lewis C. Hanserd
(Grandfather)
Odessa Byox
(Grandmother)

Grandfather from Athens,
AL

| (son) Carl | (daughter) | (son) Gregori | (son) Jocelyn |

| Steven Dion Nicholas | Duntai Tammy | Treece Javonte Jason Cheneia | Taylor Paige |

157

CPSIA information can be obtained
at www.ICGtesting.com
Printed in the USA
LVHW030631020322
712306LV00002B/231

9 781662 841330